GOD'S BLUEPRINT FOR MANKIND

AS REVEALED IN THE FEASTS OF THE LORD

BY ELLYN OLSEN

TRIUNE BOOKS AND BIBLES
1326 TENNESSEE AVE.
CINCINNATI, OHIO 45229
(513) 242-7451

BLESS ISRAEL TODAY®
NEW CITY, NEW YORK 10956

Scripture quotations are from the King James Version (KJV) and the
Revised Standard Version (RSV) of the Bible and also the Scofield
Bible (Scof.).

Cover and illustrations by Sue Gioulis of Cornerstone Arts

God's Blueprint for Mankind
©1983 by Ellyn Olsen
All Rights Reserved

Library of Congress Catalogue Card Number 83-072382
ISBN 0-913961-00-0
Printed in the U.S.A.

CONTENTS

INTRODUCTION

Before becoming a Christian, I tried many times to read the Scriptures. But they were difficult to understand and I would give up quickly. Suddenly, after giving my heart to the Lord, the Scriptures opened up to me. The Bible made sense to me and became very important in my life, as the Holy Spirit gave revelation to my spirit of God's Word.

Later in my Christian experience, Scriptures relating to the Holy Spirit took on deeper meaning and opened up a whole new understanding of God's Word to me.

In 1966, I met and married Emil Olsen. Emil was in a ministry to the Jewish people. I had come to appreciate and enjoy the Jewish people very much as a Christian. But now, being in a Jewish ministry and involved with Hebrew-Christian scholars, something really new and exciting happened to me. The Scriptures opened to me in yet a third dimension. I was seeing the Bible from a Jewish perspective.

The Bible is a Jewish book. It was written by Jewish men under the unction of the Holy Spirit about the Jewish people and their God. It is written about the Messiah who came as a Jew and about His Jewish disciples who proclaimed the Good News, not only to the Jewish race, but also to the Gentiles.

I believe, and my experience confirms, that when we see the Bible from a Jewish perspective and with Jewish understanding, even more wonderful things are revealed to us regarding God's Word.

This book is a study of the seven Jewish feasts which God gave to His people, Israel, at the time of Moses. When I first heard of the Feasts, or Holy Days, and of their prophetic meaning, I became completely fascinated. I marveled at how wonderfully and completely God had planned out the path the human race would take after its fall from Paradise to its restoration to God and back to Paradise again.

I stand amazed at how God laid out this plan so long ago in the Feasts of the Lord. There it is in the Word of God—there it is in the Feasts Israel celebrates every year—God's plan of redemption for mankind. But it can only be seen with spiritual eyes and with a Jewish understanding.

This book is not a scholarly discourse. I am not a scholar. I am simply relating to you some of the wonders and excitement I have found as God's Word regarding the Feasts came alive to me.

Emil and I are now in an independent ministry located in New City, New York, in Rockland County, 25 miles north of New York City. The ministry is called Bless Israel Today. We have had many opportunities to share this teaching on the Feasts of the Lord and about God's prophetic timepiece— Israel—with various independent groups and in churches. Each time this lesson has been given, someone has asked, "Do you have that in writing? I'd like to read something on it".

Well, here it is. I trust it will be as big a blessing to you as you read it as it has to me as I wrote it.

GOD SPEAKS THROUGH TYPES

"Therefore let no one pass judgment on you in question of food and drink or with regard to a festival or a new moon or a sabbath. These are only a shadow of what is to come; but the substance belongs to Christ."
Colossians 2:16,17 RSV

Throughout the Old Testament God spoke to His people through types. A type is a divinely planned illustration of some truth. The type may be a person, an event, a thing, an institution or a ceremonial. For instance, God again and again in the Old Testament gave types regarding His Messiah. That is, a person, or thing, etc. in the Old Testament was a type or picture of the Messiah to come. This was done so that when the Messiah would come, He could be recognized by those spiritually attuned.

For example, Joseph, the son of Jacob, was sold by his brothers to slave traders. He was made a slave in Egypt and suffered many injustices before rising to power as second in command next to Pharoah. Joseph is a type of Messiah, the suffering servant. There will be more about Joseph later.

Boaz, whose story is found in the Book of Ruth in the Bible, is also a type. Boaz became the husband of Ruth by redeeming, or paying the price for, the land of Naomi (Ruth's mother-in-law). Because he redeemed the land, it was Boaz's responsibility to take Ruth as his wife to raise up children for Ruth's deceased husband, Boaz's near kinsman. This was according to the law (Leviticus 25:25-34 and Deuteronomy

7

25:5-10). Boaz then became the "kinsman redeemer". Jesus is God yet He became a man, our kinsman in the flesh. He became our Redeemer by paying the price for our sins on the cross.

This is not to say that these men did not live and that their stories are just that—stories. They did live. But God fore-ordained their lives in such a way that they became types to point the way to the Messiah.

Jesus Himself referred to an Old Testament type when the scribes and pharisees asked Him for a sign. He said, "An evil and adulterous generation seeketh after a sign, and there shall no sign be given to it, but the sign of the prophet, Jonah; for as Jonah was three days and three nights in the whale's belly, so shall the son of man be three days and three nights in the heart of the earth." (Matthew 12:39 & 40 KJV)

Now Jonah could have obeyed God the first time and gone to Nineveh as he was instructed. But he didn't. And God in His foreknowledge knew Jonah wouldn't go as he was told. So God sent a big fish to swallow up Jonah for three days and three nights. Thus, good old Jonah became a type of Messiah Who would spend three days in the grave.*

God also used "things" as types. The tabernacle in the wilderness with all of its detail and splendor is a type of Messiah Jesus. God gave the master plan for the tabernacle to Moses. The colors—purple, blue, scarlet and white—each mean something. The wood and the metals, the fabrics and the precious stones are all significant of some fact or characteristic of the Messiah which was to come.

There is another type which I feel is so beautiful because it shows us the Godhead. When Abraham wanted a wife for his son, Isaac, he sent his servant to go to his kindred and find a bride. The servant is a type of the Holy Spirit going out in the land to find a bride for the Son. Isaac, the son, became a type of Messiah, the Son of God; Rebekah, the bride of Isaac, is a type of the Bride of Christ (the Church); and Abraham is a type of God the Father.

The Bible has many types to help our understanding, not only about Messiah, but about many Bible truths, if we will only use our spiritual eyes. Jesus often spoke in parables (or

---

*In Jewish reckoning, any part of day is judged a day. Jesus was crucified and buried on Friday and rose from the dead on Sunday. Friday and Sunday each count as one day.

types) to give a lesson and to open understanding. And many times He said, "He who has ears to hear; let him hear". This did not mean that the people could not hear. Jesus meant that they should listen with spiritual ears and spiritual understanding.

The Feasts A Type

There is a great deal of interest in prophecy at this time in history. There are also many teachings today regarding God's redemptive plan for the world and the end times. I do not claim to be a scholar nor do I claim to know all of the details, but within myself I have no question about God's overall plan for His creation. The plan of which I speak is God's redemptive plan that began at Jesus' first coming and will culminate in His second coming. Colossians 2:16 and 17 tells us that the Feast days and Sabbath were a shadow or type of things to come. Since learning about Jewish people and, in particular, learning about the Seven Feasts of the Lord, God's perfect all encompassing plan for mankind has been made real to me.

The redemptive plan of God has also been simplified for me through the Feasts. At times, as a new Christian, I would get confused about the sequence of events regarding the end times. However, knowing and understanding the Feasts of the Lord and their prophetic significance has helped me keep the major end time events straight in my thinking.

The Feasts of the Lord were given by God to the Jewish people through Moses. The Feasts are kept by the Jewish people to this very day. However, they are not kept the way God directed at the time of Moses. Each one of the feasts was to be celebrated in Jerusalem. Each one required a sacrifice at the Temple. The Jewish people have not been able to sacrifice at the Temple since 70 A.D. when the Temple was destroyed by the Romans.

Through the centuries rabbis have substituted tradition and ritual for sacrifice in the celebration of the Feasts. The interesting and exciting thing to me is that even in these rabbinical embellishments of the Feasts we can see spiritual truths. I will be sharing some of these fascinating truths with you as we study each feast.

We live in a very heavily Jewish populated area. Many of the Jewish people we know are Reformed Jews. This means that religiously speaking, they are not trying to live by the law or to keep the feasts strictly. We also have the very Orthodox and Hasidic Jewish people in our county who tenaciously hold on to their tradition. They try to live by the law, as interpreted by their rabbis, as closely as they are able. These people will faithfully keep the Feasts of the Lord as the rabbi prescribes.

These feasts are also meant to speak to those of us who know the Lord. And so I am going to share with you here the truths God was teaching His people Israel through the types of the Feasts of the Lord.

God's Blueprint

On the facing page I have drawn "God's Blueprint for Mankind". The graph on top shows the "blueprint" in church terms. That is, the words used for each event noted on the graph are familiar to you if you have heard prophecy spoken of in church circles.

The "blueprint" on the bottom shows the same graph, but with the feasts and related Jewish terms listed. It is the same "blueprint". The graph on the bottom simply uses the Feasts God gave His people at the time of Moses instead of the more contemporary terms on the top graph.

You will see in the following chapters that the prophecy which is typified in the first four feasts has already been fulfilled. These first four feasts were fulfilled at Jesus' first coming. We are now in the Church Age. It is only during the Church Age that the Jewish people are set aside as a nation (not as individuals). God has been dealing with the nations (the Gentiles) as well as Jewish people during the Church Age. When God is ready to resume His plan for the Jewish people as a Nation, He will remove the Church from the scene. Then, the Lord will once again be one on one with His people, Israel.

As we now approach the end of time, we see God again dealing with His people Israel. The most obvious sign of this is the return of the Jewish people to the land of their fathers. They are returning for a divine rendezvous. God's dealing with the Jewish people is a clue to us that the Lord is winding up His

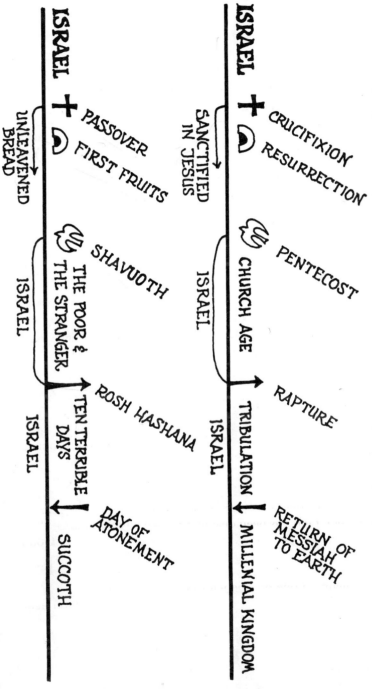

GOD'S BLUEPRINT FOR MANKIND

master program for mankind. The final three feasts are about to be fulfilled.

The seven Feasts of the Lord deal with God's redemptive plan for the earth as we know it now. The final three feasts, yet to be fulfilled, will take place here on earth just as the first four feasts were fulfilled here. Then God will establish a new heaven and a new earth.

God's redemptive plan was established before the foundation of the world. He has given us a glimpse of it in the types of the Feasts. I believe that as you read these pages prayerfully, you will be greatly blessed by God's revelation to man in the Feasts of the Lord. *These Feasts are God's Blueprint for Mankind.*

THE SABBATH

In Leviticus chapter 23 we read about the Seven Feasts of the Lord. Though these feasts appear in other portions of scripture, they are not always all mentioned together. In Leviticus chapter 23, they are all named and their fixed order in the calendar year is declared.

These feasts are literal feasts which the Jewish people keep to this day. However, they are also prophetic in nature. A close look at these feasts with prophetic understanding from the Lord, gives us a clear picture of God's plan of redemption for the world. In just this one chapter, Leviticus 23, we can see the death of Messiah, His resurrection, the Church Age, the rapture and the millenial kingdom—a beautiful overview of God's love and grace to the world—to those who believe.

There are seven feasts prescribed in Leviticus 23 starting with the Passover in verse 5. Verse 4 leads into the Feasts with these words, "These are the appointed feasts of the Lord." However, Leviticus 23:1-3 also prepares us for the feasts that follow. Let us read Leviticus 23:1-3:

> *The Lord said to Moses, "Say to the people of Israel, 'The appointed feasts of the Lord which you shall proclaim as holy convocations, my appointed feasts, are these. Six days shall work be done; but on the seventh day is a sabbath of solemn rest, a holy convocation; you shall do no work; it is a sabbath to the Lord in all your dwellings.'" (RSV)*

Bible scholars tell us that there are just Seven Feasts of the Lord. As I mentioned above, the feasts begin in verse 5 with the Passover. The Sabbath is not included in the feasts. Yet in verse 2 just before God lists the feasts for His people, the Bible says, "my appointed feasts are these" and then proceeds to tell us about the Sabbath. It would almost appear that the Sabbath is included in the Feasts, yet it is not. Again, verse 4 of Leviticus 23 says, "These are the appointed feasts of the Lord" and starts with the Passover. Why? Why is the Sabbath mentioned and not included? Is there a conflict here? No. I believe God is trying to show us something. But what? I'm sure there is some reason for the Sabbath being mentioned here at the beginning of the chapter on the Feasts.

I puzzled over these thoughts for several days. Then it occurred to me that the Sabbath is a very important feast, but it is not one of the annual seven feasts. That is, the Seven Feasts of the Lord are each celebrated only once during the calendar year. The Sabbath is the one feast that occurs frequently— every seven days. The Sabbath is on the seventh day of the week.

The seventh day is called the Sabbath because the Lord God said, "Six days shalt thou labor and do all thy work; but the seventh day is the sabbath of the Lord thy God; in it thou shalt not do any work, . . . for in six days the Lord made heaven and earth, the sea, and all that in them is, and rested the seventh day; wherefore, the Lord blessed the sabbath day, and hallowed it." (Exodus 20:9-11 KJV)

There is an exciting reason for the Lord prefacing the Feasts of the Lord with the Sabbath—a reason that will speak to our hearts. Taking a closer look at the Sabbath from several perspectives will help us to understand why it is mentioned first in this portion of scripture in Leviticus and yet is seemingly not a part of the feasts.

Sabbath Among the Orthodox Jews

The word "sabbath" in the Hebrew means "to rest". It does not mean Saturday or Sunday. It really gives the meaning of "no work". The Orthodox Jewish people to this day will do absolutely no work on the Sabbath. The wives will cook their

Sabbath meal on Friday before sunset* so that they need not cook or even light the stove on Sabbath.

The men will do no work on the Sabbath. They will not even drive a car. To start the engine of their car would be to start a fire since they are igniting the engine with a spark. Exodus chapter 35 verse 3 says, "you shall kindle no fire in all your habitations on the sabbath day". Therefore, lighting a fire of any kind, even starting the car is forbidden.

We have a Gentile Christian friend who lives in a very Orthodox area near us. One cold, rainy Friday evening there was a knock on his front door. Upon opening the door he saw a Hasidic Jewish man (ultra-Orthodox) standing there in his traditional garb of black, with his black hat and peyous (long side curls).

The Jewish man first asked our friend if he were Jewish. Our friend replied that he was not. In that case, the Orthodox man replied, "It's a cold damp night. I have a small baby at home. It is the Sabbath and our house is cold. Could you come and turn up the thermostat a few degrees?" Of course, our friend went with him and did as he was asked.

The point of this story is that even in our day and even with a small baby and a cold house, this Jewish man in the New York City suburbs would not turn up his thermostat. Again, to turn up the thermostat even just a degree would be to start a fire and the Bible says, "you shall kindle no fire in all your habitations on the sabbath day."

By the way, you may wonder why the Jewish man asked our friend if he were Jewish before he made his request. You see, the Orthodox man would not want to cause even a liberal (reformed or conservative) Jewish brother to violate the law. He would not request a Jewish man or woman to do something that would break the law. But a Gentile would be different. The Gentiles are not under the law.

I feel it would be wise at this time to give a breakdown of the various religious groups within Judaism and a brief general description. What I say here will indeed be general as there will be all kinds of variations within each group.

There are three main groups in Judaism—the Reformed, the Conservative and the Orthodox.

*The Jewish day starts at sundown. Sunset Friday night is when the Jewish Sabbath begins. It ends at sundown the next day.

The Reformed Jews are very contemporary in their dress and are usually not very religious. They do not generally keep the Kosher laws (the dietary laws) except perhaps for the sake of their parents. Most Reformed Jews do not attend synagogue regularly. They will usually go to synagogue for High Holy Days and they will celebrate the Passover.

The Conservative groups are still modern in their dress, but they are more likely to keep the Kosher laws. They will be more religious, though they still may not go to synagogue regularly. The men will wear yarmulkas in the synagogue and the women will cover their heads during a service.

Emil and I attended a Conservative synagogue in a community near us several times. Marge, a Hebrew-Christian friend, and her children went with us on our first Sabbath Eve visit. In the foyer of the synagogue there was a table with two small cardboard boxes on it. One box contained yarmulkas and one box held lace head coverings complete with bobby pins for the women. Most of the members of the synagogue brought their own head coverings, but the boxes were there just in case someone forgot or visitors would come.

As we went through the double doors into the sanctuary, Marge leaned over and whispered to me that I shouldn't be carrying my purse in the synagogue on Shabbat (Sabbath). Embarrassed by my ignorance, I tried to camouflage my purse under my coat which I slung over my arm. The people were extremely friendly to us and no one at least appeared to notice my purse. The evening turned out well, but it was one time I was literally left holding the bag.

Recently, I discussed the incident at the Conservative synagogue with Marge. "Why is it the women don't carry purses in the synagogue on the Sabbath?", I asked. "You know, I'm really not sure", Marge replied. "I just know you don't do it". She might have added, "Tradition, that's all tradition".

Many things Jewish people do and don't do are a result of tradition. A good deal of the time they, like Marge, are not really sure why they do certain things. They just follow their traditions because that is the way it is. If you think about it, perhaps we Gentiles are controlled by our traditions in much the same way. In any case, much of Jewish life is dictated by rules, regulations and traditions (in varying degrees depending upon how observant the individual Jewish person is).

While the Conservative Jewish people may try to keep some of the laws and traditions of Judaism, they are not nearly as strict as the Orthodox.

The Orthodox are easier to spot in a crowd than their more contemporary Jewish counterparts. The Orthodox men will wear a yarmulka (skull cap) or some other head covering at all times. They will also wear the long side curls (peyous) in front of their ears. Some of the Orthodox men will tuck the peyous behind their ears so they cannot be readily seen. The Orthodox women will also wear a head covering—usually a head scarf. The women never wear slacks or shorts. Their dresses may be quite modern, though extremely modest in design.

The Orthodox will strictly observe the Kosher laws. My husband, Emil, and I visited an Orthodox husband and wife some time ago. The wife proudly showed me her enormous kitchen. The kitchen had to be enormous to accommodate her two sets of everyday dishes, her two sets of good dishes and her two sets of Passover dishes plus two stoves, two sinks, two refrigerators.

Why? Because the Kosher laws say you must not mix meat and milk together. To a Conservative Jewish family this may mean simply not serving meat and milk at the same meal. To the Orthodox this means not using dishes for milk products when they've been used for meat products. Therefore the Jewish mother will have a set of "milk" dishes and a set of "meat " dishes. She will not wash a "meat" dish in a "milk" sink or store a "meat" dish in a "milk" refrigerator. And, of course, these rules go for the flatware as well. Why all of this trouble to keep meat and milk separate? Because the Bible says, "Thou shalt not seethe a kid in his mother's milk" (Exodus 23:19).

The dietary laws go beyond mixing meat and milk. Kosher also refers to the way the animals are slaughtered. Furthermore, certain foods on grocery shelves have special markings which indicate they are "Kosher". These foods are Kosher because they are prepared under rabbinical supervision and in a kosher, or proper, manner. There is much more to the Kosher laws, but I will not go into it here for the space is limited and I don't believe it would serve a purpose.

The Kosher laws are only part of the precepts—Biblical and rabbinical—that weigh the Orthodox Jewish people down. They try to live by them all. As the Jewish people say, "It's not easy to be a Jew".

The Hasidic Jews are the Ultra-Orthodox. They are readily identified by their dress. The men wear black; their hats will vary from group to group. Some are furry (in the winter, of course), some are tall black hats. They always have their heads covered, many times wearing a yarmulka under their hats. The Hasidic men wear beards and their hair short with long side curls in front of the ears. The hair in front of the ears of the Orthodox and Hasidic men is never cut. From infancy this hair is left untouched because the Bible says, "You shall not round off the hair on your temples or mar the edges of your beard." (Leviticus 19:27)

The Hasidic women wear colors other than black. Their sleeves are long and so are their skirts; the necklines are high. They also wear wigs that cover their shaven heads. I understand the heads of the women are shaved at the time of marriage to show submission to their husbands. The clothing of the Hasidic men and women is made of pure fabrics such as linen or wool.

The Hasidic, too, keep the Kosher laws and attempt to keep all of the laws of Moses. Like the Orthodox, the Hasidic spend many hours a week in their synagogues. The men are the religious leaders in the family and it is the men who spend most of their time in the synagogue. When the women attend the synagogue services, they are separated ·from the men by a partition.

The Hasidic are under the strong influence of the particular rabbi of their sect. The rabbi is revered by his people. He interprets the law and directs his people in every area of their lives.

The Hassidic remain an extremely separate people. Yiddish is their "native" language; they maintain their own schools. All of these things keep them from outside influences.

The Orthodox and Hasidic tend to live in clusters near their synagogues. There are many reasons for this. For one thing, they have their own community with their own customs, language, schools, foods, etc.; they live amongst their own. The synagogue also plays a big role in their daily lives and thus they live close to it. Another reason for living near the synagogue is that on the Sabbath and other holy days, they cannot drive their cars as was mentioned before. Neither are they allowed to walk very far on the Sabbath. The disciples in Acts 1:12 walked a Sabbath day's journey. That is only about 2000 cubits or a little more than a ½ mile. Even today, the Orthodox and Hasidic Jews will only walk a Sabbath day's journey. Therefore they live close to their synagogues.

When I was in the hospital with our last baby, Emil and I struck up a conversation with an Orthodox Jewish woman in the Maternity Ward's lounge. Like us, she had paid for her hospital visit in advance because paying in advanced offered a savings. The advance payment plan entitled each patient to a four day stay. However, this meant release from the hospital for our Jewish friend would be on Saturday. Saturday is the Sabbath and her husband could not travel even the short distance from their home to get her, so she would have to stay until Sunday.

Speaking of the hospital reminds me of another story I heard recently. It seems everyone in our area has a favorite story to tell about the Orthodox and Hasidic people. The man who related this experience is a guard at the local hospital. He said that on the Sabbath when the Orthodox come into the hospital, they won't step on the automatic door opener. They wait until someone else steps on it and goes in, then the Orthodox person quickly scampers through behind him. The Orthodox would not want to be guilty of operating the automatic door opener on the Sabbath.

Now a good question at this point is, "Why are there Orthodox Jews at the hospital on the Sabbath to use the auto-matic doors if you say they can't drive on the Sabbath?" The answer to that is there are many groups of Orthodox and Hasidic Jews, each with a rabbi who acts as spiritual leader of his sect as was noted before. Each rabbi is well versed in the Talmud. The Talmud is a book of rabbinical interpretations of the law of Moses. Using the Talmud, the rabbis will determine what can and cannot be done regarding every phase of life. One group of Orthodox may not be able to drive at all while another can drive, but perhaps only under specific conditions, such as an emergency. Some groups of Orthodox may be able to use public transportation on the Sabbath though not being permitted to drive themselves. Others will not be allowed to drive or use public transportation at all. In any case, the lives of the Orthodox are strictly regulated by the law and their rabbi's interpretation of the law.

Sabbath Candles

There is one fire which is lit in the Jewish home on Sabbath eve. That is the Sabbath candles. There is one candle lit for each member of the family. As the candles are lit by the mother, she says a prayer in Hebrew. "Blessed art thou, oh Lord God, King of the universe, who has sanctified us with thy commandments and commanded us to light the Sabbath candles". As the mother prays this prayer, she waves her hands over the Sabbath candles in a rotating manner. It is said she is waving in the spirit of Sabbath.

As Christians, we can see some beautiful lessons in the Sabbath—lessons that show us the true meaning of the Sabbath. The Word of God tells us that Jesus is our Sabbath rest. When we put our faith and trust in Him, we rest in Him and no longer work to obtain salvation, for He is our Salvation. "So then, there remains a sabbath rest for the people of God; for whoever enters God's rest also ceases from his labors as God did from his." (Hebrews 4:9, 10 RSV)

The Sabbath candles which are lit remind us of Jesus Who is the Light of the world. He lights up the lives of all those in whom He dwells. It is also significant that the mother lights the Sabbath candles and beckons the light into the room for it was through the "seed of the woman" that the Messiah, the Light of the world, was to come. And it was through the "seed of the woman" that Jesus came into this world. Jesus is the true Spirit of Sabbath.

It was Jesus to whom the Sabbath pointed; He said, "For the Son of Man is Lord of the Sabbath." (Matthew 12:8) And so it is that the Sabbath is mentioned here in Leviticus 23 before we even get into the Seven Feasts of the Lord. Jesus is the center of each feast. In Him each feast finds its completion.

The Jewish people celebrate these feasts each year, year after year; yet, they do not understand the prophetic significance of each feast because they have failed to find their Messiah. The feasts speak of God's redemptive plan for the Jewish people and for the nations. *Jesus is that plan.*

As we look at each of these feasts in the forthcoming chapters, we will see how, as a nation, they have sadly missed the very center and meaning of each feast—Jesus, the Messiah.

THE HEBREW CALENDAR

Observe the month of Abib, and keep the passover unto the Lord thy God, for in the month of Abib the Lord thy God brought thee forth out of Egypt by night.

Deuteronomy 16:1 KJV

Before we go any further, I believe it would be beneficial to take a brief look at the Hebrew calendar. The Hebrew calendar is quite different from the Gregorian calendar which we use.

The Hebrew calendar is based on the moon, whereas the Gregorian calendar is based on the sun. The Hebrew calendar normally has twelve months. The months of the year in order are: Tishri, Heshvan, Kislev, Tibet, Shebat, Adar, Nisan (or Abib), Iyar, Sivan, Tammuz, Ab and Elul. The months are alternately 30 and 29 days long. Seven times during every 19 year period there is an extra month inserted between Adar and Nisan. The extra month is called Veadar (or second Adar). The same year that Veadar is added to the calendar, the month of Adar is given 30 days instead of 29. All of this is to adjust for the difference between the movements of the sun and moon.

Obviously the months of the Hebrew calendar and the months of the Gregorian calendar do not run concurrently. But they do correlate to a certain extent. Following is a general relationship between the two calendars:

Tishri	September - October
Heshvan	October - November
Kislev	November - December
Tibet	December - January
Shebat	January - February
Adar	February - March
Nisan (or Abib)	March - April
Iyar	April - May
Sivan	May - June
Tammuz	June - July
Ab	July - August
Elul	August - September

Another big difference between the two calendars is the year each will be representing. The Gregorian calendar records the year counting more or less from the birth of Christ. The Hebrew calendar records the year counting from creation. While I am not sure how the year was first arrived at, tradition says creation started at a moment 3,760 years and 3 months before the Christian Era. So in the winter of 1980-1981, the Hebrew year was 5741.

Most Jewish people today, when speaking of or writing a year, will use the Gregorian year simply because it is easier to use in communicating with the rest of the world. But if it is a year they are writing that is after the birth of Christ they will not use the abreviation A.D. (in the year of our Lord). Rather, they will use the abreviation C.E. meaning "Common Era". In other words, the U.S. had its two hundredth anniversary in 1976 C.E.

Most Jewish people, if they are speaking of a year before the birth of Christ (B.C.) will use the initials B.C.E. This means "Before Common Era".

If that bothers you, don't let it. I personally can agree with their logic. Why should they say "1980 in the year of our Lord" when they have not acknowledged Jesus as their Lord?

"In the First Month"

One other piece of information regarding the Hebrew calendar is essential if we are going to study the Feasts of the Lord. When we begin reading Leviticus 23:5 regarding Passover, we will see that Passover is to come in the first month of the year. "In the first month, on the fourteenth day of the month in the evening, is the Lord's passover". Passover comes in the first month of the year, the month of Nisan (also called Abib) according to the Word of God. However, the rabbis teach that there are two calendars, a religious calendar and a secular calendar. The month of Tishri is the first month of the secular calendar while Nisan is the first month of the religious calendar.

Why there are two calendars and why the first month of the year has been changed from Nisan in the spring to Tishri in the fall is unclear. As in many instances in Jewish life, when there is no concrete answer, the answer is "Tradition". Tradition says that God created the world during the month of Tishri so Rosh Hashana, or Jewish New Year, is celebrated at the beginning of Tishri, the seventh month.

As we study the Feasts of the Lord, we will, of course, follow the sequence given in the Bible which begins with Passover. Actually, God's order is necessary in understanding the Feasts and their meanings. Their meanings follow in logical sequence according to the way God laid them out in Leviticus 23 starting with Passover and ending with the Feast of Booths in the month of Tishri.

The Feasts in the Calendar

Now for a quick overview of the feasts in the year and where they fit into the Hebrew calendar.

The first feast in the Hebrew calendar (according to God's order as listed in Leviticus 23) is Passover. It is on the 14th day of the first month, that is Nisan in the spring. Passover is always very close to Easter.

The second feast is the Feast of Unleavened Bread. This feast starts immediately after Passover. Passover begins on the "fourteenth day of the month in the evening" and Unleavened Bread starts on "the fifteenth day of the same month" and lasts for seven days. Actually, today Jewish people will refer to the full eight day period which incorporates Passover and Unleavened Bread as simply "Passover" (or in Hebrew, Pesach). Sometimes some *may* refer to the two feasts as the Feast of Unleavened Bread, though I believe this is rare. In most cases, the term "Passover" is used in speaking of the eight day holiday.

In any case, the Feasts of Passover and Unleavened Bread are joined together in the thinking and celebration as one feast in the minds of most people. We will see in a later chapter that God had His reasons (prophetic reasons) for putting these two feasts so close. Together they form a beautiful picture of salvation.

The next feast in God's calendar of events is the Feast of First Fruits. Now the Feast of First Fruits does not have a fixed date for celebration. Its date will move from year to year. What *is* definite is that it falls within the week of the Feast of Unleavened Bread. It is also always on "the morrow after the sabbath". That is to say the Feast of First Fruits will always fall on a Sunday. Sunday is the morrow (or day) after the Sabbath. So, while the date will fluctuate for the Feast of First Fruits it is always set to come during the week of Unleavened Bread on Sunday. Again, we will see later the importance of this interesting fact.

While these first three feasts come in rapid succession and are actually a kind of unit, (that is Passover and Unleavened Bread follow each other one right after the other and First Fruits comes within the week of Unleavened Bread), the next feast occurs 50 days later. The Bible says, "count from the morrow after the sabbath, from the day you brought the sheaf of the wave offering; seven full weeks shall they be, counting fifty days to the morrow after the seventh sabbath". We already learned that the Feast of First Fruits came on the morrow after the Sabbath during the week of Unleavened Bread. Now God says to count from the day of the Feast of First Fruits (the morrow after the sabbath) "fifty days to the morrow after the seventh sabbath". The Feast of Shavuoth, or the Feast of Weeks, also has a floating date. The day of the celebration of the Feast of Weeks is determined upon the date of the Feast of

First Fruits, for both are celebrated on Sunday and the Feast of Weeks is fifty days after First Fruits (an indefinite date).

There is now a big lapse of time between feasts. In a sense, it is an indeterminate length of time because the date of the Feast of Weeks is so moveable. A big gap of time occurs between the Feast of Weeks and the next feast because the Feast of Weeks will usually come in our month of May and the next feast, the Feast of Trumpets, comes in September. While the first three feasts come in rapid succession with the fourth relatively close behind, we now have the large space of time before the observance of the next feast.

We will see as we get into the meaning of each feast that prophetically, the first four feasts have already been fulfilled. The final three feasts have yet to be fulfilled. Prophetically, we are living in that big lapse of time. We are now approaching the last three feasts and they too come in rapid succession.

The Feast of Trumpets comes "in the seventh month, on the first day of the month". The Feast of Trumpets is more commonly known as Rosh Hashana, or Jewish New Year.

"On the tenth day of the seventh month is the day of atonement". Just ten days after Rosh Hashana comes the Day of Atonement. This Holy Day as we will see is not really a "Feast" day at all.

Then "on the fifteenth day of this seventh month and for seven days is the feast of booths to the Lord". The Feast of Booths, or Feast of Tabernacles, comes just five days after the Day of Atonement. So it is that the last three feasts come quickly, within a period of fifteen days.

And thus ends the calendar of the Seven Feasts of the Lord. The Feast of Tabernacles brings to a close God's plan of redemption.

But for us this is just the beginning. We've just taken a bird's-eye view of God's plan. This was a little introduction to get acquainted with the Feasts and where they are located on the calendar. Now we are going to get into the finer points and see the lesson God has for us. I believe you will be as thrilled as I when you see how perfect and detailed God's plan has been from the beginning and how beautifully the Old and New Testaments mesh together.

THE FEAST OF PASSOVER

4. "These are the appointed feasts of the Lord, the holy convocations, which you shall proclaim at the time appointed for them. 5. In the first month, on the fourteenth day of the month in the evening, is the Lord's passover. 6. And on the fifteenth day of the same month is the feast of unleavened bread to the Lord; seven days you shall eat unleavened bread. 7. On the first day you shall have a holy convocation; you shall do no laborious work. 8. But you shall present an offering by fire to the Lord seven days; on the seventh day is a holy convocation; you shall do no laborious work." 9. And the Lord said to Moses, 10. "Say to the people of Israel, When you come into the land which I give you and reap its harvest, you shall bring the sheaf of the first fruits of your harvest to the priest; 11. and he shall wave the sheaf before the Lord, that you may find acceptance; on the morrow after the sabbath the priest shall wave it. 12. And on the day when you wave the sheaf, you shall offer a male lamb a year old without blemish as a burnt offering to the Lord. 13. And the cereal offering with it shall be two tenths of an ephah of fine flour mixed with oil, to be offered by fire to the Lord, a pleasing odor; and the drink offering with it shall be of wine, a fourth of a hin. 14. And you shall eat neither bread nor grain parched or fresh until this same day, until you have brought the offering of your God: it is a statute for ever throughout your generations in all your dwellings."

Leviticus 23:4-14 RSV

In this passage of Scripture, you will note that there are actually three feasts mentioned. They are the Feast of Passover (verse 5), the Feast of Unleavened Bread (verse 6), and the Feast of First Fruits (verse 10). I am lumping these feasts together because, as we noted in the previous chapter, they are celebrated together and because their prophetic fulfillment goes together. The three feasts are actually interrelated.

The first feast mentioned in this portion of Scripture is the Passover, which is the first feast to be celebrated in the Hebrew year. It is immediately followed by the Feast of Unleavened Bread. The Lord's Passover is on the fourteenth day of the month in the evening; Unleavened Bread starts on the fifteenth day of the same month. These Feasts are celebrated together over a period of eight days. Today the whole eight day period is called simply "Passover" though it is actually the combination of the Feast of Passover and the Feast of Unleavened Bread. During the eight day Passover season, the Feast of First Fruits is celebrated, but, again, it is considered part of Passover.

Passover is the celebration of God's deliverance of His people Israel out of bondage to Pharaoh in Egypt. God used Moses as their deliverer and leader. The name "Passover" comes from the last plague which God sent upon Egypt in a successful attempt to get Pharaoh to agree to let His people go. God told Moses to have each family in Goshen (where the Israelites were living in Egypt) take a spotless lamb (a lamb that was perfect, without blemish) and slay it. Each Israelite family was to take the blood of the lamb and apply it to the door posts of their home in a distinct manner. Then, the night would come when God would send the death angel to slay all of the first born in the land of Egypt. But God said, "The blood shall be a sign for you, upon the houses where you are; and when I see the blood, I will pass over you, and no plague shall fall upon you to destroy you, when I smite the land of Egypt".

So God's death angel passed over the homes of the Israelites who had applied the blood to the door posts. The first born of the Egyptians were slain. Because of this final plague Pharaoh agreed to let the Israelites go.

A Summary of Leviticus 23:4-14

While this portion of scripture in Leviticus chapter 23 doesn't say so, the Passover feast was to be commemorated every year by the sacrifice of a lamb on the evening of the 14th day of the first month. God does, however, mention the sacrifice of the Passover lamb in many other scripture portions. The lamb was to be slain "in the evening at the going down of the sun, at the time you came out of Egypt". (Deuteronomy 16:6) They were to eat all of the sacrifice. None was to be left until morning.

Passover is followed immediately by the Feast of Unleavened Bread on the fifteenth day of the first month. This feast was to last seven days. During those seven days absolutely no leaven was to be in the house—no leaven was to be eaten.

On the day after the Sabbath which came during the seven days of the Feast of Unleavened Bread, the Jewish people were to bring the sheaf of the first fruits of their harvest as a wave offering before the Lord. This is the Feast of First Fruits.

What does all of this mean in God's prophetic calendar of events? How are these feasts celebrated today? Let us first look at the observance of Passover today and from there we can see its significance to us. I feel I should mention at this point that in the remainder of this chapter I will be describing a typical Orthodox family's celebration of Passover. While the basics of the traditional feast are the same from home to home, there will also be variations in many of the details.

Passover In Today's Jewish Homes

Today the Passover lambs are no longer sacrificed as God commanded them to be. Immediately, you can see that the Feast of Passover, as it was prescribed in the Word of God, is not celebrated. The Passover lambs cannot be sacrificed because there is no Temple in which to sacrifice them. It was at the Temple in Jerusalem, and there only, that the Passover lambs were to be sacrificed. The Temple was destroyed by Titus in 70 A.D. and since that time, the Feast of Passover as it was meant to be is only a hope.

But, it is still remembered today as Jewish families gather

together on Passover eve to praise God for redeeming His people Israel from the land of Egypt. The Jewish family will eat their Passover meal with unleavened bread and bitter herbs which God commanded them to do. However, the all important sacrificial lamb is not part of the service.

Today, instead of preparing a lamb for sacrifice during the four days before Passover as they were commanded to do, the Jewish mother will work to prepare the home for the Feast. In fact, these preparations sometimes start as much as one month before Passover season. The home is made spotless. Every bit of leaven is removed from the house as God commanded: "Seven days shall ye eat unleavened bread; even the first day ye shall put away leaven out of your houses; for whosoever eateth leavened bread from the first day until the seventh day, that soul shall be cut off from Israel." (Exodus 12:15 Scof.) Bread, cereal, cake, all of these must be given away or thrown out. Many times a Gentile friend or neighbor is the beneficiary of the command to rid the house of leaven.

Before the Passover service can begin, Father must make a final inspection of the house. Father will take a wooden spoon, a large feather and a napkin. He, and probably his youngest son, search the house carefully from top to bottom. They are looking for leaven. Though Mother has been very careful to clean the house thoroughly of leaven, she has left a few crumbs on the windowsill or table for Father to find. Father finds the crumbs. He sweeps them with the feather into the wooden spoon. He wraps the crumbs, spoon and feather into the napkin and goes down to the synagogue where a fire is burning. Here the father throws the spoon, crumbs, feather and napkin into the fire. All of the other Jewish fathers are arriving at the synagogue too, in order to cast their napkins containing the leaven into the fire.

Then Father returns home where he prays, "Blessed art thou, O Eternal, our God! King of the Universe, who hast sanctified us with thy commandments, and commanded us to remove the leaven.

"All manner of leaven that is in my possession, which I have seen and which I have not seen, which I have removed and which I have not removed, shall be as nought and accounted as the dust of the earth."

At home on Passover evening, the family begins to gather. It can become a very large gathering as a whole family may come together at Grandfather's house with all of the grandchildren. The oldest male present, Grandfather or Father, becomes the master of the feast. It is the master of the feast who leads the family in prayers and worship and who reads through the Hagadah. The Hagadah is a book which gives the order of service for the Passover celebration. It gives all of the instructions for the Passover service and includes all of the prayers. The Passover service will start at sundown and last until after midnight. This can be four to six hours. The family will read completely through the Hagadah.

As the family takes their places at the dinner table to start the service, they will see before them a small cup filled with wine at each place setting. The drinking of the wine is important to the Passover. Each person's cup will be filled with wine four times throughout the Passover service. There is a title given to each filling. They are: the Cup of Sanctification, the Cup of Praise, the Cup of Redemption and the Cup of Elijah. The drinkings of each of these cups set the order of the service and also help us to remember the various portions of the Passover celebration.

Also on the table is a Seder plate. The word "Seder" means "order". Often the Passover service is referred to as a Seder service. The Seder plate has six items on it which also help to order the service and which add significance and understanding to the redemption of the Israelites from the land of Egypt.

There is a shankbone of a lamb on the plate. This reminds the people of the Passover lamb which is supposed to be sacrificed in the Temple each year. As there is no longer a Temple and sacrifices are no longer made, the Jewish people have only the shankbone as a remembrance.

A hard boiled egg is placed on the Seder plate. This reminds the people of the daily sacrifice in the Temple for the sins of the Israelites. These daily sacrifices were made each morning by the priests. But, again, since the Temple was destroyed, the sacrifices have not been made. One explanation for the egg on the Passover table is that an egg is laid every morning just as the sacrifice was to be made every morning. So the egg is on the Seder plate as a reminder of the daily sacrifice.

There is a small dish of salt water on the Seder plate to remind the people of the tears that were shed by the Israelites
when they were slaves in Egypt. Also, there is parsley. The
parsley represents life. At one point in the Seder service the
parsley is dipped into the salt water and eaten. This shows us
that life is immersed in tears.

Also on the Seder plate are an onion and horseradish. This
is because God told the Israelites to celebrate the Passover Feast
with unleavened bread and bitter herbs, the latter of which are
represented by the horseradish and onion. During the Seder service, everyone takes a piece of unleavened bread, dips it into the
horseradish, and eats a bite of the unleavened bread with a nice
big mound of horseradish on it. This is done to bring tears to
the eyes — and it really works!

There is also a dish of Haroseth on the Seder plate.
Haroseth is a sweet tasting dish of chopped apple, raisins, nuts,
cinnamon, sugar mixed together with a little wine to make a
sweet tasting paste. We are told by the rabbis that the Haroseth
represents the mortar which the Israelites made as slaves in
Egypt. "But, Rabbi", a dear Jewish man may ask, "why is the
Haroseth so sweet when the work was hard, bitter work for
us?" "That is right", says the rabbi, "but our work was sweet
unto us becaused we knew our redemption was drawing nigh."

As you will note from the two "quoted" statements above,
both the Jewish man speaking and the rabbi use the term "us"
and "we" in referring to the children of Israel who were slaves
in Egypt. The Talmud says, "In every generation, every Jew
should see himself as if it were he who was redeemed from
slavery in Egypt". Therefore, throughout the Seder service the
words "we" and "us" are used as the people relate to that time
3,500 years ago when they (as a people) were redeemed. They
are identifying with this redemption.

At every Passover table there is a place set for a special
guest. This place is designated by a special wine cup and is
usually at a table setting closest to a door. But no one sits in this
chair. This place at the Passover table is reserved for the
prophet Elijah. The Bible used by most Jewish people only
consists of the first 39 books of our Bible — that is, the Old
Testament. The last book in the Old Testament is the book of

Malachi. The prophet Malachi in chapter 4 verse 5 says, "Behold, I will send you Elijah the prophet before the great and terrible day of the Lord comes". The Jewish people are expecting Elijah to come and usher in the Messiah, so a place is reserved at the Passover table for Elijah in the hope that this year the prophet will come and prepare the way for the expected Messiah.

As the family takes their seats at the table to begin the Passover, the mother of the house lights the candles and gives the blessing in Hebrew, "Blessed art thou, O Lord God, King of the Universe, who has sanctified us by thy commandments and commanded us to light the candles of Yom Tov (Feast Day)". This is the only part the mother plays in the service, religiously speaking. Mother takes her place at the table and then Father begins the service.

In an Orthodox home, the father, or the master of the feast, will be wearing a white robe (kittle) and a high white hat (mitre). The robe shows the father's priestly position in the home and the mitre shows his kingly position. In a more contemporary Jewish home the father (and the other males) will simply wear a yarmulka and a prayer shawl. The father reads a prayer in Hebrew from the Hagadah thanking God for His love which provided Sabbaths for rest, festivals for joy and most particularly the Feast of Passover, "the time of our freedom". The prayer goes on to invite *all* who are hungry and in need to come and take part. After this prayer everyone drinks the wine in his cup for the first time. This is the Cup of Sanctification.

This prayer and the drinking of the cup of wine opens the Seder service. As I stated before, the service is a long one. The Hagadah is a large book and the Orthodox Jews will go through it from cover to cover on Passover evening. For our purposes here, I am only going to mention some high points which I believe will be of interest as well as informative and will speak to us spiritually.

On the Passover table we see only unleavened bread or matzoh. Matzohs are large flat "crackers" made of flour and water without yeast or leavening. Sometimes they are square and others are made round. Each matzoh is called a loaf. No leavened bread can be eaten during the eight days of the

Passover season. There is plenty of unleavened bread available for all to eat. There is also a unique arrangement of three matzohs on the Passover table. These matzohs are arranged so that they are together in one cloth container, yet separated from each other by other pieces of cloth. It looks something like a cloth bag with three separate compartments. The father picks up the bag and reaches into the middle compartment. He pulls out the middle loaf of unleavened bread and breaks it in two. He places half of the matzoh back into the bag and cautiously wraps the other half in a napkin and hides it away. He tries to hide it inconspicuously because before the service is over the children must find the broken matzoh and bring it back to the father. The child who finds it gets a prize.

Just before everyone drinks the second cup of wine, which is the Cup of Praise, the master of the feast holds his cup of wine up and drops out ten drops of wine. As he does this he names the ten plagues which God brought upon Egypt at the time of Moses—blood, frogs, lice, wild beasts, cattle plague, boils, hail, locusts, darkness, death of the first born. He then leads his family and guests in giving praise to God for His redemption and deliverance. Now, each one drinks from his cup which has been filled for the second time—the Cup of Praise.

It is at this point, after the second cup, that a sumptuous dinner is served. It is like Thanksgiving, only twice as much food. There is gefillte fish, matzoh ball soup and all the goodies a Jewish Mamalah likes to prepare for her family and guests to make joyous hearts.

After dinner, one of the children retrieves the broken piece of matzoh which has been hidden away. The father takes this piece of matzoh in hand and breaks it into small pieces and gives each person present one piece. They take it and eat it. Then the father takes his cup filled with wine for the third time (the Cup of Redemption) and leads each one at the table to do likewise, and they all drink from their cups.

Now the wine cups are filled for the fourth time (the Cup of Elijah). A little boy gets up from the table and goes to the door near to Elijah's chair and looks out. He is looking for the prophet Elijah. But, he does not see Elijah. He returns to the table and the father prays a final prayer which ends with the hope that perhaps next year they will celebrate Passover in Jerusalem. No one drinks from his cup this fourth time. Instead of this happy feast ending on a joyous note, there is a sense of sadness and unfulfillment as Elijah has not come to usher in the Messiah who will give them the total redemption they seek.

But God has provided full redemption, and we will see it as we discuss the true meaning of this Passover feast in the following pages... PASSOVER—ITS FULFILLMENT.

PASSOVER — ITS FULFILLMENT

"...Do you not know that a little leaven leavens the whole lump? Cleanse out the old leaven that you may be a new lump, as you really are unleavened. For Christ, our paschal lamb, has been sacrificed. Let us, therefore, celebrate the festival, not with the old leaven, the leaven of malice and evil, but with the unleavened bread of sincerity and truth."

I Corinthians 5:6-8 RSV

The Passover service, though a beautiful service, receives its true beauty in its fulfillment. God performed a truly great miracle in redeeming the Jewish people out of the land of Egypt. But the redemption from the land of Egypt and the Passover feast pointed forward to an even greater redemption. Just as the Jewish father begins the Passover service by praying and inviting *all* who are hungry and in need to come—so the greater redemption is for *all*. The Jewish father does not specify Jew or Gentile in his prayer and neither does Jesus in His invitation. Jesus said, "Come to me, *all* who labor and are heavy laden, and I will give you rest." (Matthew 11:28)

In the Scripture quoted above from the first letter to the Corinthians in the New Testament, we see that God, through the Apostle Paul, was pointing out the significance of the Passover and the Feast of Unleavened Bread as it relates to us as individuals. Paul says, "Cleanse out the old leaven that you may be a new lump, as you really are unleavened."

Just as the father in a Jewish home must rid that home of leaven before the Passover, we are told to cleanse out the old leaven. The Bible teaches us that leaven is a type of sin, "the leaven of malice and evil". When Adam and Eve sinned by doing their own thing and disobeying God, sin came into the human race. We are all affected. "Do you not know that a little leaven leavens the whole lump?" (I Corinthians 5:6) Each one of us has been born in sin because sin, like leaven, has permeated the whole lump (the human race). Father must clean out every crumb of leaven from the home before the Passover can begin. But how can we clean out every crumb of sin from our lives? The Passover feast gives us the simple answer to, what seems, this most difficult question.

In the previous chapter, I pointed out that on the Passover table there is a special arrangement of matzoh—three loaves of matzoh separated yet within one container. Each loaf is a large flat square or round sheet—a kind of giant cracker.

Matzoh is used on the Passover table and throughout the entire eight day period because it is unleavened bread. You could say it is a type of sinless bread. Matzoh is always made with lines of little prick marks and dark lines or stripes baked into the loaf or cracker. This type of sinless bread with its prick marks and stripes reminds us of several verses of Scripture: "they have pierced my hands and feet" (Psalms 22:16 RSV), ". . .with his stripes we are healed". (Isaiah 53:5) Jesus said, "I am the bread of life." (John 6:51)

The father, at the Passover table, picks up the special arrangement of matzoh and breaks the middle loaf and hides it away. Rabbis have many thoughts as to why there are three loaves on the Passover table in such a special arrangement. Some rabbis will say that the three loaves represent the Priests, the Levites and the Camp of Israel. Others say they represent Abraham, Isaac and Jacob. But, of course, the question is, what did Isaac do that he should be broken? Some rabbis will just give a quicky answer like "tradition, that's all, tradition". But as believers in Jesus, the Messiah, we can see the triune God represented at this Jewish feast. Three in one—Father, Son, and Holy Spirit. The Son—the middle loaf—is broken and buried— hid away. The hidden piece of unleavened bread is

The Cross of Blood on the Door of every Israelite Home

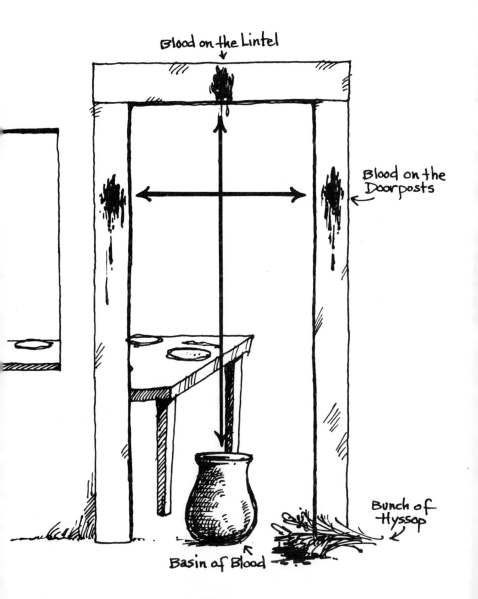

Blood on the Lintel

Blood on the Doorposts

Bunch of Hyssop

Basin of Blood

brought back to the table at the third cup in the feast. The Son was brought back to life—resurrected—on the third day.

As Jesus celebrated the Passover with His disciples the night he was betrayed, He came to the third cup, the cup after supper, "And he took bread, and gave thanks, and broke it, and gave unto them, saying, 'This is my body which is given for you; this do in remembrance of me'. Likewise also the cup after supper, saying, 'This cup is the new testament in my blood, which is shed for you'". (Luke 22:19-20 KJV)

Jesus' death and resurrection and the redemption He provides is the fulfillment of the Passover feast. But how can we receive that redemption? Certainly Jesus died for all, but not all have found that redemption. What must we do? The answer to this question can be found in the story of the Passover itself.

When the Israelites were still in Egypt in the land of Goshen, God told them He was going to bring one final plague upon the land. This plague would make Pharaoh let God's people go. This tenth plague was the death of the first born in every family; no one would be spared. No one, that is, unless he followed God's instructions. God did provide a way, but only one way, for the first born to be saved.

Each family was to take a lamb—a spotless lamb—and observe that lamb for four days. It had to be perfect. But that perfect lamb alone was not enough to save that family from the plague of death. That lamb had to die. His blood had to be shed. But even that was not enough; the blood had to be collected in a basin. Then the father of the house back in the land of Goshen took a bunch of hyssop, and with the basin of blood sitting in front of the door to the house, the father dipped the hyssop into the blood and struck the lintel. Then he struck the one door post with the blood and then the other. As the blood dripped down from the lintel to the ground and each door post oozed with the fresh blood of the lamb just applied, you can see that the father made the sign of a cross of blood on the door of his home. Anyone in that house that night would be spared from the death angel, because God said, "When I see the blood, I will pass over you". When God's death angel saw the cross of blood at the door of the house, he passed over that home. There was only one way for the first born to be saved from death. There is only one way for us to be saved from eternal death. That is God's way.

God said by the prophet Malachi that Elijah would come and prepare the way for the Messiah. "Behold, I will send you Elijah the prophet before the great and terrible day of the Lord comes. And he will turn the hearts of fathers to their children and hearts of children to their fathers, lest I come and smite the land with a curse." (Malachi 4:5,6 RSV) That is why even today the Jewish people have a place set for Elijah at their Passover table. They are waiting for Elijah to come and point them to the Messiah. But Elijah has come already. Jesus said of John the Baptist, "This is he of whom it is written, 'Behold, I send my messenger before thy face, who shall prepare thy way before thee'" (Luke 7:27). John came "in the spirit and power of Elijah" (Luke 1:17). It was John who saw Jesus walking one day and said of Him, "Behold the lamb of God who takes away the sin of the world!"

Jesus lived a perfect life, but His perfect life does not save us. Jesus, like the Passover lamb, had to die. But that still does not save us. The blood of that sacrifice on the cross must be applied to our heart's door.

Jesus' death on the cross is there for all—Jew and Gentile. It's a free gift of eternal life to you and me. If the death angel had seen a cross of blood on Egyptian doors that night thousands of years ago, he would have passed over their houses too. But the Egyptians didn't believe and did not apply the blood to the door as God prescribed. If any Israelite did not apply the blood—death would strike their home. You see, life was available to all and death was a sure thing, but each person had to believe and apply the blood. They had to have faith and obey God's way of salvation to have life. And that's the way it is with Jesus. Life eternal, life abundant is there. Death is certain. But to receive life, we must receive Jesus and accept His gift of eternal life.

The Israelites in Egypt were told to eat all of the lamb on that Passover eve. None of it was to remain. God also said that at subsequent Passover feasts the lamb was supposed to be finished—completely consumed. Jesus said, "I am the living bread which came down from heaven; if any one eats of this bread, he will live forever...Truly, truly, I say to you, unless you eat the flesh of the Son of man and drink his blood, you have no life in you; he who eats my flesh and drinks my blood has eternal life, and I will raise him up at the last day. For my flesh is food indeed, and my blood is drink indeed. He who eats my flesh and drinks my blood abides in me, and I in him. As the living Father sent me, and I live because of the Father, so he who eats me will live because of me.'' (John 6:51-57 RSV)

We do not literally consume Jesus' flesh and blood, but we must take Him into our lives. As food which we eat—meat and drink—becomes part of us, so Jesus must become part of us. He must live in us and through us as Lord of our lives. Then we will have abundant life and the redemption of soul from sin that God promised us back at the time of Moses.

If you don't know Jesus, God's Passover Lamb, personally —if you haven't had a personal life changing encounter with God through Jesus, His Son, you can right now. Jesus is waiting and ready to welcome you into God's family—His family of Jews and Gentiles who have given their lives over to Jesus and trusted Him for salvation. You can apply His blood to your heart's door right now. If you want to receive Jesus, just bow you head and pray:

Dear God of Abraham, Isaac and Jacob, I know I was born in sin and have continued to sin against you all of my life. I'm sick of my life as it is. I want a new life. Thank you, Jesus, for shedding Your blood for me. I accept Your sacrifice on my behalf and I ask You to come into my life and be Lord of my life from this day on. In Your Name I ask it. Amen.

THE FEASTS OF UNLEAVENED BREAD
AND FIRST FRUITS

*"To the church of God..., to those sanctified in
Christ Jesus, called to be saints together with all those
who in every place call on the name of our Lord
Jesus Christ, both their Lord and ours:"*
                                        I Corinthians 1:2 RSV

The Feast of Unleavened Bread is the very next feast mentioned in Leviticus 23 (read Leviticus 23:6-14). It follows the
Feast of Passover in Scripture. Passover is mentioned in verse 5
of Leviticus 23 and the Feast of Unleavened Bread immediately
follows in verse 6. Unleavened Bread also follows Passover
immediately in its celebration. Passover is in the evening of the
14th day of the month of Nisan. The Feast of Unleavened Bread
falls on the 15th day of the month of Nisan.

As I mentioned in the chapter on Passover, even though
the eight day holiday is called Passover, in reality it is the Feast
of Unleavened Bread. Passover cannot really be celebrated the
way it was prescribed by God because the Passover lambs can
no longer be sacrificed at the Temple. Instead, the Passover
traditions, as handed down by the rabbis for centuries from one
generation to another, are kept at the traditional Passover
dinner served on Passover eve. Eating unleavened bread at the
Passover table is one of the commandments God gave the
Jewish people regarding Passover. God told Moses on the night
of Passover the Israelites "shall eat the flesh (of the lamb) that
night roasted; with unleavened bread and bitter herbs" (Exodus

12:8). Unlike the Passover lamb, the unleavened bread and bitter herbs are still a part of the Passover feast.

Also, eating unleavened bread rather than leavened bread for the eight days of what we call Passover today is a big part of the spring holiday season. Even among some of the reformed and non-religious Jewish people today, eating only matzoh during the week of Passover season is a must. A few years ago we had a young Jewish friend of our son come over for the day. It was during Passover week. When we had lunch I put cold cuts on a platter. I knew Mark and his family well enough to know he did not come from a religious family or a kosher home. So I felt free to include ham on the platter. I knew Mark could always pass it up and it would not offend him. Mark had eaten ham before anyway even though it is not kosher.

I did remember, however, that in the past, Mark always ate matzoh during Passover. Therefore I made sure matzoh was on the table for him. Sure enough, Mark wouldn't touch the nice fluffy leavened bread on the table, but reached immediately for the unleavened bread (the matzoh). I smiled to myself as I saw Mark gingerly serve himself the ham on top of his matzoh.

While Mark and his family stick to the tradition of eating only unleavened bread during Passover week even though they are not kosher, many liberal Jewish people will not even do that. They may just have the matzoh on the table on the first night of the Passover celebration. It is strictly a matter of personal conviction and, of course, tradition.

It is interesting to note that there are three feasts which God commanded the Jewish males to celebrate "in the place which he shall choose" (or Jerusalem). We find this command in Deuteronomy 16:16. "Three times in a year shall all thy males appear before the Lord thy God in the place which he shall choose: in the feast of unleavened bread, in the feast of weeks and in the feast of tabernacles". Three times a year the Jewish males were compelled to make the trip to Jerusalem to commemorate the feasts.

This is very significant. We must realize that the Jewish males were in Jerusalem at the time of Jesus' death on the cross. Most likely their families were also with them. We read in the Gospel of Luke chapter 2 verses 41 through 52 the account of

Jesus and His family going to Jerusalem for Passover when He was 12 years old. They went with a large company of people "kinsfolk and acquaintances". So it would seem that when the Jewish males went up to Jerusalem at the command of God for those three feasts their families went also.

The Jewish men would appear in Jerusalem to sacrifice their Passover lambs and then remain there for the week of the Feast of Unleavened Bread which followed immediately. That means that all of these men were in Jerusalem to witness the earthshaking events which took place at that time; namely Jesus' death and subsequent resurrection.

Prophetically Speaking

God specified that the Feast of Unleavened Bread come immediately after Passover for a very good reason. The prophetic meaning of this feast gives us a vivid picture of what happens at the moment we accept Jesus as our Passover Lamb. As we learned in the previous chapter, leaven speaks of sin. Unleavened bread is therefore a type of sinless bread. The Feast of Unleavened Bread speaks of the sinless life we live in Jesus the Messiah. Not that we are without sin. As we will see in the next chapter, sin is still a part of our life. But in Jesus we are sanctified. Sanctified is a good theological word that means *to be* made holy, *to be* freed from sin, *to be* consecrated. It's not what we do, it is what has been done for us. The two little words "to be" give the sense of being done for us. "To be" made Holy, for instance, means we are made Holy. We do not make ourselves Holy. Jesus died for us and when we accept His completed work on Calvary as our Passover Lamb, we are *immediately* set free from sin, just as the Feast of Unleavened Bread *immediately* follows Passover. There is no waiting period —no gap of time to see if we can live a good life or do a good deed. We become holy instantly because Jesus has made us that way.

We know from Bible scholars that the number seven refers to completion. There are seven days of Unleavened Bread. In Jesus we not only become holy, but we are complete. Before I accepted Jesus, I felt empty. A kind of deep void was in my life. Everyone is born with a compartment in his soul—a place for

God to dwell. But we are born in sin. Since man first desired to do his own thing and disobey God, the human race has been blighted by sin. The compartment for God has remained empty because God is holy and we are sinners. Therefore our lives seem empty no matter what we do to fill the emptiness.

When Jesus came into my life, I entered into a relationship with God and I became a complete person. I could have that relationship with a holy God because I had been made holy. I had become sinless in Jesus and God came in and filled my life.

Let me mention again that it is not what I'm doing that makes me sinless. I sin every day, I'm sorry to say. But I have to. make that confession of sin in my life because it's true and the Bible says, "If we say we have not sinned, we make him a liar, and his word is not in us." (I John 1:10 RSV) Someone has put it this way; when we accept Jesus as Lord, He steps between us and God. Therefore when God looks on us, He doesn't see old sinful me or you; He sees us through Jesus. The sin is filtered out. We have been made free of sin. Therefore, the Feast of Unleavened Bread centers around Jesus and His work of cleansing us from sin and making us a new creation. "Therefore, if any man be in Christ, he is a new creature; old things are passed away; behold, all things are become new". (II Corinthians 5:17 KJV)

The Feast of First Fruits

> *"But in fact Christ (Messiah) has been raised from the dead, the first fruits of those who have fallen asleep. For as by a man came death, by a man has come also the resurrection of the dead. For as in Adam all die, so also in Christ shall all be made alive. But each in his own order: Christ the first fruits, then at his coming those who belong to Christ."*
>
> *I Corinthians 15:20-23 RSV*

You will note in Leviticus 23:11 that the Feast of First Fruits is to be celebrated "on the morrow after the sabbath the priest shall wave it". The Sabbath as we know is Saturday. I realize I have said that a few times before, but so often as

Christians we think of the Sabbath as Sunday. We are reading the Bible which is a Jewish book and in it the Sabbath is Saturday. So the morrow after the Sabbath, or the day after the Sabbath, would be Sunday. The Feast of First Fruits was to be celebrated during the week of the Feast of Unleavened Bread and it was to be celebrated on Sunday (the first day of the week). Unlike the previous Festival days, the Feast of First Fruits has no set date. It will vary from year to year depending on which day Passover falls. First there will be Passover, then the following day will begin the Feast of Unleavened Bread. Then within that week on the day after the Sabbath will be the Feast of First Fruits.

Today, the Feast of First Fruits doesn't appear to be as important as it might have been back in the Old Testament days. At that time, the Jewish people were to have a wave offering of the sheaf of the first fruits. And on that same day they were to offer sacrifices—a lamb, cereal offering, etc. But today it is impossible for these offerings to be made. I asked one Orthodox rabbi what he did to celebrate First Fruits and his answer was that he simply gave a special blessing on that feast day.

Though the Feast of First Fruits may not seem so terribly important to the Jewish people today, its significance is very important to the Christian. Our whole Christian faith revolves around the prophetic meaning of this feast. "But now is Christ risen from the dead and become the first fruits of them that slept." (I Corinthians 15:20 KJV)

The Lord, through the Apostle Paul, even went so far as to say, "if Christ has not been raised, then our preaching is in vain and your faith is in vain." (I Corinthians 15:14 RSV) Jesus' resurrection from the dead (the first fruits of them that sleep) is the pivotal point of our faith as Christians. The Feast of First Fruits is a very important feast as far as its prophetic fulfillment. Other religions have had great leaders. All of these leaders are dead. In most cases you can even be directed to their graves. But the Christian "religion"*, like no other religion, has a living resurrected leader. His grave is empty. And because He lives we will live eternally also.

God's timing is always perfect. Jesus, as the Passover Lamb, was crucified on the exact day at the exact hour that the

---

*I detest the word "religion" when it comes to true Christianity. To those who really know the Lord Jesus personally, theirs is not a dead, traditional religion, but a living, active, vital faith.

Passover lambs were to be sacrificed that year. He was not crucified the day before or the day after, but on the proper day. And at the precise moment, Jesus gave up the ghost (His life).

It was on the first day of the week, "the morrow after the Sabbath", that Jesus rose from the dead. "But on the first day of the week, at early dawn, they went to the tomb. . . but when they went in, they did not find the body of the Lord Jesus". (Luke 24:1-3 RSV)

Jesus was raised from the dead according to God's perfect plan on the first day of the week following Passover and during the Feast of Unleavened Bread. In other words, Jesus was literally raised on the morning of the Feast of First Fruits. Jesus *is* the Feast of First Fruits!

THE FEAST OF SHAVUOTH

*"And you shall count from the morrow after the
sabbath, from the day that you brought the sheaf of
the wave offering; seven full weeks shall they be,
counting fifty days to the morrow after the seventh
sabbath; then you shall present a cereal offering of
new grain to the Lord. You shall bring from your
dwellings two loaves of bread to be waved, made of
two tenths of an ephah; they shall be of fine flour,
they shall be baked with leaven, as first fruits to the
Lord. And you shall present with the bread seven
lambs a year old without blemish, and one young bull,
and two rams; they shall be a burnt offering to the
Lord, with their cereal offering and their drink offerings, an offering by fire, a pleasing odor to the Lord.
And you shall offer one male goat for a sin offering,
and two male lambs a year old as a sacrifice of peace
offerings. And the priest shall wave them with the
bread of the first fruits as a wave offering before the
Lord, with the two lambs; they shall be holy to the
Lord for the priest. And you shall make proclamation
on the same day; you shall hold a holy convocation;
you shall do no laborious work; it is a statute for ever
in all your dwellings throughout your generations."*
Leviticus 23:15-23 RSV

The Feast of Shavuoth is the Feast of Weeks. It is so called because it is celebrated seven full weeks after the Feast of First Fruits, and seven weeks is in reality "a week of weeks". The Feast of Shavuoth or "weeks" comes by its name rightly.

Shavuoth is one of the three feasts which required that all Jewish males go up to Jerusalem to offer sacrifices. The other two feasts which required this trip to Jerusalem are the Feast of Unleavened Bread and the Feast of Tabernacles.

Shavuoth is considered a harvest festival and the Book of Ruth is read aloud in the synagogues today to celebrate this feast. The Book of Ruth speaks of harvesting in ancient Israel. Tradition also says that Shavuoth is the celebration of the day the Ten Commandments were revealed to Moses.

What could this harvest festival possibly have to do with God's redemptive plan for mankind? Pentecost is a word with which you may be more familiar. Pentecost is another name for Shavuoth. The name Pentecost comes from the Greek word for "fifty" because this feast comes fifty days after the Feast of First Fruits, "Count from the morrow after the Sabbath, from the day that you brought the sheaf of the wave offering. . . counting fifty days to the morrow after the seventh sabbath." Pentecost, like the Feast of First Fruits, was always on Sunday. It was on "the morrow after the seventh sabbath". The Feast of Shavuoth and the Feast of First Fruits do not have fixed dates. They are the only two feasts that do not have a set date.

We know from our New Testament Scriptures that "when the day of Pentecost had come, they (the disciples) were all together in one place" and the Holy Spirit came upon them and they spoke in tongues.

We also know that "there were dwelling in Jerusalem Jews, devout men from every nation under heaven". Why were there devout male Jews from every nation under heaven in Jerusalem? Because it was the Feast of Shavuoth ("the day of Pentecost") and they were there as God required of them under the law to sacrifice in the Temple.

I might also add that God planned it that way. God wanted these men in Jerusalem on the day the Holy Spirit descended upon the disciples of Jesus. It was all part of The Plan. These devout Jewish men from every nation heard the commotion when the disciples began to speak in other tongues and they were amazed and wondered. Then the Apostle Peter got up and, with the new power he had just received from on high, he spoke a Spirit-filled message that cut the hearts of these men.

When Peter finished speaking, these devout men who had come to Jerusalem for Shavuoth asked Peter and the others, "Brethren, what shall we do?" They were told to repent and be baptized and receive the gift of the Holy Spirit. The Bible tells us about 3,000 souls were added to the Church that day.

These devout born again Jewish Christians from every nation under heaven then went back to their homes transformed and proclaimed the Gospel of their new found Messiah. The Church was born!

Hebrew-Christian scholars and others today will tell you that the Feast of Shavuoth or Pentecost which was given to the Jewish people at the time of Moses speaks of the birth of the Church. In light of what we've just seen from Scripture, this seems quite obvious.

It is interesting to me that today the Jewish people consider Shavuoth the celebration of the giving of the Ten Commandments. The giving of the law at the time of Moses really contrasts with the giving of God's grace and the Holy Spirit on the day of Pentecost. The one—the law—speaks of works, mitzvahs or good deeds as the Jewish people say. The other—the day of Pentecost at the time of the disciples—speaks of the love of God being poured out upon His people and setting them free from the bondage of sin.

You will note that in Leviticus 23 at the Feast of Shavuoth two loaves of bread were to be brought from each dwelling. These loaves were to be made a wave offering. They were also to be baked *with* leaven.

The two loaves represent Jew and Gentile together. The fact that this wave offering is two loaves of bread and not sheafs of grain, as in the Feast of First Fruits, shows it represents a homogenized group—that is the Church. The Church was not to be made up of Jews alone, as it was in its first few decades. Nor is the Church only Gentiles, as so many think today. The Church is a new creation of God. The middle wall of partition is broken down and the Jewish people and the Gentiles together are one in Jesus. Speaking of the Church, God says, "Here there cannot be Greek and Jew, circumcised and uncircumcised, barbarian, Scythian, slave, free man, but Christ is all, and in all." (Colossians 3:11 RSV)

As was mentioned in the chapter on Passover, leaven in the Bible is a type of sin. These two loaves which were offered as a wave offering were specifically to be baked with leaven in them.

God is showing us a truth here, a truth that should make a lot of us breathe easier.

As I pointed out in the chapter on the Feast of Unleavened Bread, as believers in Jesus the Messiah, we are living sanctified lives. That is, we are made holy and set aside for the Master's use. However, we don't want to get the idea that *we* must live a holy life. The important word in that last statement is "we". You and I are unable to live a holy life. We are subject to sin. The more we try to live good, sinless lives the worse it will get.

I well remember when, as a new Christian, I decided (out of my gratitude to God for saving me) that I would live a life that would be pleasing to Him. I worked in a public office at the time and handled public complaints and problems. I loved the Lord so much, I wanted to show my customers His love by not getting angry with them. (If you have ever handled public complaints you will understand the challenge I was facing.) At the same time, God would see my love for Him as I lived the way I believed He wanted me to live. Each day I tried not to get upset with my customers and each day I failed at my goal earlier and earlier in the day. Every time I failed by becoming angry, I would become frustrated. And every time I became frustrated, I would get more angry. It was a vicious cycle.

During this same period of time, I was reading through the New Testament for the first time in my life. I had just read through the Book of Acts. I "fell in love" with the Apostle Paul and the great man of God he was for the Lord. What a person! What a missionary! What faith! What zeal! He was terrific!

God's timing is perfect. Just as I was in the week of my frustrating failures for the Lord, I came to Romans 7. Paul, that great man of God wrote, "For I know that in me dwelleth no good thing; for to will is present with me, but how to perform that which is good I find not. For the good that I would, I do not; but the evil which I would not, that I do...O wretched man that I am! Who shall deliver me from the body of this death?'' (Romans 7:18, 19, 24 Scof.) As a young Christian, I couldn't believe the words I was reading from the pen of this great apostle. He felt just like me! I was totally unable to do anything good no matter how hard I tried.

"Oh, God", I cried out, "What is the Answer. Who can help me?" The Lord spoke to me these words. "If you could live without sin, you wouldn't need Jesus."

Paul cried out to the Lord almost the same question I did. "Who shall deliver me from the body of this death?" And God's answer to Paul (and to us) is, "There is, therefore, now no condemnation to them who are in Christ Jesus, who walk not after the flesh, but after the Spirit." (Romans 8:1 Scof.)

I discovered that I need Jesus every day, not just the day I met Him for the first time and asked for the forgiveness of my past sins. I need to keep under His cover 24 hours a day. In myself I sin. I don't want to, but I do. I thank God that there is no condemnation to me as long as I stay in Jesus. "If we confess our sins, He is faithful and just to forgive us our sins, and to cleanse us from all unrighteousness." (I John 1:9 KJV)

That was one of the first lessons I ever learned from the Lord as a Christian. And I thank God for it. I have never had a hang up about living a good life since; I just don't try any more. The Lord helped me to find that true freedom in Him. "For freedom Christ has set us free; stand fast therefore, and do not submit again to a yoke of slavery." (Galatians 5:1 RSV)

Now if you're sitting there reading this and saying, "Well, I've never had that problem. I don't become frustrated at trying to live a holy life. I live my life pretty well for the Lord. Why, I don't smoke, I don't drink, I don't go to movies, I don't watch TV, I don't wear jewelry, I don't dance, I don't...''. Well, that may be all well and good. But check your attitude. Don't forget the Pharisees were religious, moral people too. The only problem they had was they were self righteous. That made them much less than God wanted. In their self righteousness they didn't need Jesus.

The key words to living a truly holy life are "trust" and "love". Trust in the Lord Jesus, His saving grace, and His sanctifying power to keep us. When we have that trust and faith, we will cease to live our Christian life in our own strength.

I believe that as we continue to live in Jesus and He in us, we will live a holy life just because we love Him and His love lives in us. We don't have to know the law or rules. We don't have to make up self imposed regulations. As Jesus lives in us, His love will motivate us.

Through love and trust we have another cycle. Not a vicious cycle, as I mentioned before, but a precious cycle. First comes our trust. We trust Jesus for saving us and keeping us. Then we love Him because of His love which saves and keeps. Because of our love for Him, we trust Him more, and in so doing we are released from the burden of responsibility for our sanctification. We become free in our souls before God and man and we are happier and better able to live our lives the way God intended.

And when we fail (as we surely will, because we continue to dwell in flesh until we go to be with our Lord), well, we don't have to worry or become frustrated. Jesus knows all about it. He lived in human form and He's aware of our problems. When we come to Jesus and repent and confess our sins, He forgives. Not only that, but I believe He delights in our need and dependence on Him.

Please don't misunderstand. I am not saying we should or can go out and willfully sin and then come running back and ask forgiveness. I don't believe it works that way. After all, we can't repent if we're not truly sorry. And we're not truly sorry when we've purposely turned from God with the attitude, "He'll take me back when I'm ready". Jesus knows the heart of each person. In our Christian walk, we should become more and more in love with Jesus and more and more at one with Him. In that condition, we would not willfully sin against Him.

You and I need not feel condemnation when we sin. Conviction, yes, but not condemnation. Conviction is when the Holy Spirit speaks to our hearts and tells us we did wrong and need to ask forgiveness. It is conviction which brings us to our knees before God, not condemnation. Condemnation tells us God is angry with us and cannot forgive us one more time. Condemnation drives us away from God. It is conviction and not condemnation which comes from the Lord.

God doesn't expect His Church to be sinless—not yet anyway. And understanding that fact should be a help and blessing to us all. If you know the Lord, you can relax and enjoy your life in Him. If you don't know Jesus yet, you can be assured that you don't have to be perfect to become a Christian. God told the Israelites regarding the Feast of Shavuoth, the loaves "shall be baked with leaven". God was saying at the time of Moses exactly what I've seen written on many bumper stickers: "Christians aren't perfect, they're just forgiven".

THE POOR AND THE STRANGER

"And when you reap the harvest of your land, you shall not reap your field to its very border, nor shall you gather the gleanings after your harvest; you shall leave them for the poor and for the stranger: I am the Lord your God."

Leviticus 23:22 RSV

This Scripture is right in the middle of Leviticus 23. Leviticus 23 is entirely about the Feasts of the Lord. Yet this portion of Scripture is not about a feast. It does not refer to the previous Feast, the Feast of Shavuoth, nor does it have anything to do with the Feast to come, the Feast of Trumpets. It really appears to have nothing to do with this chapter at all. If your Bible has the paragraphs noted, you will see that this one verse is a paragraph all by itself.

Now I believe that *all* Scripture without exception is inspired by God. After all, if we finite, fallible human beings start picking out what we believe is God inspired and what we believe is not inspired, where do we end? Besides, the Bible itself says, "All scripture is inspired by God and profitable for teaching, for reproof, for correction, and for training in righteousness, that the man of God may be complete, equipped for every good work." (II Timothy 3:16, 17 RSV) So what does this verse in the middle of the Feasts of the Lord mean?

I know what some Bible scholars believe it means. I have personally accepted this meaning because it fits the overall plan of God for His creation as I believe the Bible teaches. I have also accepted this meaning because I feel a witness of the Spirit that it is so.

Of course, how I feel in the Spirit is not enough to satisfy someone else. So I pondered this thought and asked the Lord just how to explain and express teaching regarding Leviticus 23:22. It occurred to me that the Book of Ruth could help shed some light and understanding on this Scripture.

The Kinsman-Redeemer

As I mentioned in the introduction to this book, the Lord God used types in the Old Testament to speak to the Jewish people. These types presented pictures of people and events to come. Most particularly these types represented and pointed the way to the Messiah. Boaz, in the Book of Ruth, was a type of the kinsman-redeemer.

Boaz was a near kinsman of Naomi, Ruth's mother-in-law. Naomi and Ruth were both widows. Naomi had some land which she needed to sell. Boaz, as her close relative, redeemed the land for her. He also took upon himself the responsibility of raising up children for his deceased relative, Ruth's husband. All of this was according to Old Testament law (Leviticus 25:25-34 & Deuteronomy 25:5-10).

Jesus is our Redeemer for He redeemed the world with His blood. He became an eternal sacrifice for sin. And Jesus is our kinsman. He is the God-man. Jesus is God. He took on the form of man. He was flesh and blood just like you and me. He came to earth in the form of a man that He might be tempted as we are. Yet He overcame temptation and lived a perfect life. As the perfect Lamb of God — yet very much a man — He died for all men. Because Jesus was our kinsman according to the flesh (human), He was able to pay the price for our sin on the cross in our place. He became our redeemer. "If, because of one man's trespass (Adam), death reigned through that one man, much more will those who receive the abundance of grace and the free gift of righteousness reign in life through the one man Jesus Christ. Then as one man's trespass led to condemnation for all men, so one man's act of righteousness leads to acquittal and life for all men. For as by one man's disobedience many were made sinners, so by one man's obedience many will be made righteous." (Romans 5:17-19 RSV)

Now let's look at Ruth. Ruth was a Moabitess. That is she was a Gentile. Ruth had accepted the God of Israel, for she said to her Jewish mother-in-law, Naomi, "your people shall be my people, and your God my God". (Ruth 1:16 RSV) Ruth is a type of the Church. Ruth became the bride of Boaz, her kinsman redeemer. The Church is the bride of Messiah Jesus, her Kinsman-Redeemer.

Long before Ruth ever knew Boaz, she married one of Naomi's sons in the land of Moab. After a while, Ruth became a widow. She went with Naomi, also a widow, back to Bethlehem, Naomi's hometown. There, in Bethlehem, Ruth tried to provide for her mother-in-law. In the beginning of the second chapter of Ruth, Ruth did not yet know Boaz. To get food for Naomi and herself, Ruth went into the fields of Boaz to glean among the ears of grain. When Boaz saw her and found out who she was, he told Ruth not to go into any other field but his. He would see to it that she had enough grain from the gleanings of his field. She would also be safe in his field for he ordered the young men who worked for him not to molest her. Ruth was shocked that Boaz should be so kind to her. She said to him, "Why have I found favor in your eyes, that you should take notice of me, when I am a foreigner?"

In answering her, Boaz said, "...and a full reward be given you by the Lord, the God of Israel, under whose wings you have come to take refuge." Later, at mealtime, Boaz said to Ruth, "Come here, and eat some bread, and dip your morsel in the wine". This sounds very much like a part of the last supper of Jesus and our communion service today. Ruth is very much a type of the Church.

In Leviticus 23:22 we read that the border of the fields and the gleanings of the harvest were to be left for the poor and the stranger. Ruth was a poor stranger (a foreigner, as she said to Boaz) who needed to glean the fields for food. And that's exactly what some Bible scholars tell us about this strange paragraph in Leviticus. It speaks of the Church Age — that period of time when the new creation of God would go forth in the power of the Holy Spirit to bring in a harvest for the Lord.

Why isn't the Scripture in Leviticus 23:22 more explicit regarding the Church Age? Why is it so mysterious? I don't really know. We do know that the Old Testament never speaks directly of the Church Age. It only alludes to the Church Age in very abstract terms, such as this Scripture in Leviticus. The Apostle Paul states in Ephesians 3 verses 1-12 that to him was revealed the mystery of the Church. God, for reasons known only to Him, chose to veil many truths in the Old Testament. And the Church was one of them. There is a little saying that goes:

The New Testament is in the Old concealed,
The Old Testament is in the New revealed.

Certainly, in the lesson of the Feasts of the Lord, we see the truth of this saying.

This verse in Leviticus 23 verse 22 does not refer to a feast as the other verses do. I believe this is because the Feasts are exclusively or primarily dealing with the Jewish people. Even at the birth of the Church (Pentecost) the main characters were all Jews. The apostles and disciples and the onlookers were all Jews from all parts of the then known world.

As we will see from the feasts to be discussed in succeeding chapters, they also center around the Jewish people.

The Church is a new creation of God. It is a combination of Jew and Gentile together making up a new people called by God to love Him and serve Him. The "stranger" whom God speaks of in Leviticus 23:22 refers to the Gentiles. God says, "Wherefore, remember that ye, being in time past Gentiles in the flesh, who are called Uncircumcision by that which is called the Circumcision in the flesh made by hands—That at that time ye were without Christ, being aliens from the commonwealth of Israel, and strangers from the covenants of promise, having no hope, and without God in the world. But now in Christ Jesus ye who once were far off are made near by the blood of Christ." (Ephesians 2:11-13 Scof.) Until the Church Age God dealt primarily with Israel as a nation. The Gentiles were aliens, strangers from the promises of God. The Church Age is a time when God deals with *all* peoples. It is a time for the ingathering of Gentiles as well as Jews—anyone who has taken refuge under the wings of the Lord, the God of Israel.

An Indefinite Period of Time

As I mentioned in the chapters on the Feast of First Fruits and the Feast of Shavuoth, these feasts have no definite date. Their celebration depends exclusively on when Sunday comes during the week of Unleavened Bread. On that Sunday, as I explained before, the Feast of First Fruits will be celebrated. That Sunday could be the 16th of the month of Nisan or the 17th, 18th, etc., throughout the seven days of the Feast of Unleavened Bread.

Then 50 days are counted from that Sunday (the Feast of First Fruits) to the Feast of Shavuoth. That means that Shavuoth also has a moveable date because it is dependent upon the date on which First Fruits falls. I am trying to make this uncomplicated (I hope I'm succeeding). It is very important because since Shavuoth has an indefinite date, that means this time period in Leviticus 23:22 which represents the Church Age is also an indefinite period of time. The Church Age *is* an indefinite period of time. We don't know how long God will continue to deal with the Church before He takes her out. Jesus, in speaking to the church at Sardis, warned, "If, therefore, thou shalt not watch, I will come on thee as a thief, and thou shalt not know what hour I will come upon thee." (Revelation 3:3 Scof.)

So we can see that even in this little paragraph there is a big story—the Church. The Church was born in the last feast—the Feast of Shavuoth or Pentecost. Then God began dealing with all nations drawing out a new people for Himself. The Church Age will be a time of much harvesting in the fields of the world. But the Church Age will end. I believe that end will be very soon. The Jewish people as a nation will once again be in the center of God's activity here on earth.

The Jewish people are even now returning to the land of their Fathers; Israel is a nation once more. God brought them to their land and He is keeping them there against tremendous odds. Israel is a nation completely surrounded by a host of enemies who are committed to drive her into the sea. Israel has already been through many wars with her enemies, but God has kept her and made her victorious. God said, "He who scattered Israel will gather him, and will keep him as a shepherd doth his flock." (Jeremiah 31:10 RSV) God is already dealing with Israel as a people. And that dealing of God with His Ancient people will usher in the next feast—the Feast of Trumpets.

THE FEAST OF TRUMPETS

"And the Lord said to Moses, 'Say to the people of Israel, In the seventh month, on the first day of the month, you shall observe a day of solemn rest, a memorial proclaimed with blast of trumpets, a holy convocation. You shall do no laborious work; and you shall present an offering by fire to the Lord.'"

Leviticus 23:23, 24 RSV

"For the trumpet will sound, and the dead will be raised imperishable and we shall be changed." (I Corinthians 15:52b)

"For the Lord himself will descend from heaven with a cry of command, with the archangel's call, and with the sound of the trumpet of God. And the dead in Christ will rise first; then we who are alive, who are left, shall be caught up together with them in the clouds to meet the Lord in the air; and so we shall always be with the Lord." (I Thessalonians 4:16-17 RSV)

The sounding of the trumpet to the Hebrew Children was very important. It was used to sound an alarm. It was also used to gather the people together. In Leviticus 23 we are told that on the Feast of Trumpets, the trumpets are to sound and there is to be a holy convocation.

The Feast of Trumpets today is considered Jewish New Year or Rosh Hashana. Rosh Hashana means "head (or first) of the year". God specifically said the month of Nisan is to be the first month of the year and the Passover the first feast of the year. However, the rabbis teach that the trumpets usher in the

New Year. Rabbis, of course, are aware that Passover is in the first month according to the Word of God and that Passover is in Nisan. So, as I stated in the chapter on "The Hebrew Calendar", they teach there are two calendars—a religious calendar and a secular calendar. Rosh Hashana, therefore, is the first feast of the New Year on the secular calendar, thus making Tishri the first month of the year. Tradition says that God finished the creation in the month of Tishri.

Rosh Hashana is a very solemn Feast day. It is a time of soul searching. Some Orthodox groups have a special ceremony at which they symbolically cast their sins into the river. Jewish people from all three groups of Judaism go to their synagogues on Rosh Hashana for services and prayer. The trumpet or shofar (ram's horn) is sounded in every synagogue. Jewish New Year cards are sent to family and friends. It is also traditional to dip an apple in honey and eat it. This signifies the wish for a sweet New Year.

To help us get a clear understanding of this feast and what it means to the world and God's plan of redemption, I feel we need to understand what is believed by the Jewish people regarding the ten days after Rosh Hashana. The feast which follows Rosh Hashana is the Feast of Yom Kippur, or Day of Atonement, which comes ten days after Rosh Hashana. These ten days are important days to the Jewish people; they are known as the "Ten Terrible Days".

For the ten days following Rosh Hashana when Jewish people greet each other, they say in Hebrew, "May your name be inscribed for life". These words are also on the Jewish New Year cards. It is believed that during these "Ten Terrible Days" God is in heaven deciding who will live in the New Year and who will not. These are dreaded days for the Jewish people. During these ten days they perform many mitzvahs (good deeds) in order to try to influence God's decision. I believe God has put this understanding regarding these ten days into the hearts and teaching of the Jewish people.

As already indicated by the Scripture quoted from I Thessalonians 4, the Feast of Trumpets foreshadows the rapture of the Church. The true invisible Church of Jesus, the Messiah, will be gathered together to a great feast in heaven (a holy convocation). This will be a glorious time of victory. A shedding of sinful nature for once and for all. That is, we will be changed from our fleshly body which causes us to sin against God, to a new, heavenly body. "Lo! I tell you a mystery. We shall not all sleep, but we shall all be changed, in a moment, in the twinkling of an eye, at the last trumpet. For the trumpet will sound, and the dead will be raised imperishable, and we shall be changed. For this perishable nature must put on the imperishable, and this mortal nature must put on immortality." (I Corinthians 15:51-53 RSV) Those who know the Lord Jesus will be together with Him in heaven and will fellowship together one with the other.

This will be a direct fulfillment of Jesus' prophecy that He would come for the Church. He said He would go to His Father's house where there are many mansions. He will prepare a place for us there. Then He will come for His Church and receive her to Himself so that "where I am you may be also". (John 14:1-6)

Now that the true Church has been taken up out of the earth to be with her Lord, what will happen to those who are left behind? Jesus said, "For then there will be great tribulation, such as has not been from the beginning of the world until now, no, and never will be." (Matthew 24:21 RSV)

The Bible teaches that for seven years after the Church has been removed from the earth, there will be a devastating time of wars, natural and supernatural calamities and hatred of man to man in the world. It will be a time of sorrow and suffering such as this world has never seen before.

There has always been suffering and persecution in this world. There have been sufferings of individuals; there have been sufferings of peoples and nations. This has not changed. It is the same today. But Jesus said the Tribulation will be a time of *great* tribulation such as has never been and never will be. The Tribulation is a very distinct period of time in the history of man. There are at least three characteristics of the Tribulation which make it unique. One characteristic is God's personal dealings with the Jewish people as a nation (more about this later). The second is the revealing of the anti-Christ to the world (this will be covered later also). The third characteristic is the pouring out of God's wrath upon this world of sin.

There are some who believe the Church will have to go through the Tribulation. But the Bible doesn't teach this. The books of I and II Thessalonians speak much about the end times. In I Thessalonians God twice tells us that we as Christians are to be saved from His wrath. "...and to wait for his Son from heaven, whom he raised from the dead, Jesus who delivers us from the wrath to come." (I Thessalonians 1:10 RSV) "For God has not destined us for wrath, but to obtain salvation through our Lord Jesus Christ..." (I Thessalonians 5:9 RSV)

Just previously, I stated that many people have had to go through sufferings and persecutions during the thousands of years of civilization. Christians have gone through these persecutions, too, without being delivered. So why does God say we are not appointed to wrath? Why would He choose to deliver Christians from the Tribulation and not from the other tribulations of life? The answer to that question is that during the Tribulation God will be pouring out His wrath on a sinful world. The persecutions that Christians and others have had to endure in the past (and are enduring and will endure) have been man's inhumanity to man. These persecutions have actually been Satanic attacks on the human race in general and the Church and the Jewish people in particular.

The Bible shows us, however, that every time God has dealt out justice upon this evil world, He has removed the righteous. For instance, "Noah found grace in the eyes of the Lord". Noah and his family were shut safely in the ark when God destroyed the world. Lot and his family, too, were removed from Sodom when God was going to shower it with fire and brimstone.

Christians are "Children of God". God may allow His children to go through trials and tribulations, and He will go along beside each one to comfort and keep. But God is not going to pour out *His* wrath on *His* children. Even as human parents, we may allow our children to live through a particular problem, knowing that they will grow and mature by it. But, if we are half way normal and caring, we will not abuse them or inflict wounds upon them. Certainly our heavenly Father would do no worse to His children. "If you then, who are evil, know how to give good gifts to your children, how much more will your Father who is in heaven give good things to those who ask him!'' (Matthew 7:11 RSV)

The Bible tells us in no uncertain terms that the Tribulation is the wrath of God. ''(men) said to the mountains and rocks, Fall on us, and hide us from the face of him that sitteth on the throne, and from the wrath of the Lamb; For the great day of his wrath is come, and who shall be able to stand?'' (Revelation 6:16-17 Scof.) ''Go and pour out on the earth the seven bowls of the wrath of God.'' (Revelation 16:1 RSV)

So while Christians have gone and are going through persecutions (and perhaps will go through persecution in the U.S. as well), we have not experienced the wrath of God. Nor will we, for in I Thessalonians chapter 4, it speaks of the Rapture of the Church. Jesus will descend from heaven and the dead in Him (that is those who died as followers of Jesus) will rise first. Those who are alive at His coming will also be caught up to meet the Lord in the air. This is the gathering of God's people, Jew and Gentile, who have accepted Messiah, Jesus. This gathering will remove the righteous of God from the wrath of God to come and God says, ''Therefore comfort one another with these words''. When we realize the degree of devastation which will be upon the earth during the Tribulation, the assurance of the Rapture is indeed a comfort.

In the previous chapter we learned that each of the feasts centers on the Jewish people. Now that the Church has been taken out of the earth God will once again deal with His Ancient people Israel. Though all people will go through great distress, sorrow and hardships, even death, the Jewish people will experience even greater sufferings. The Jewish people will feel the effects of the wrath of God just as all peoples of the world will. The wrath of God will manifest itself in volcanic eruptions, earthquakes, famines, droughts, etc., as well as supernatural cataclysmic phenomena.

However, most of the suffering brought upon the Jewish people will be from their fellow man. Now that the restraining influence of the Church has been removed from the earth all hell will literally break loose. Anti-Semitism will be rampant. The Jewish people will again be the scape goat for mankind. Jealousy, rage and greed for the wealth of the land and its strategic position will cause the nations of the world to come against the nation of Israel. Jewish people in all parts of the world will also be caught up in the wake of this anti-Semitic fury. This is known as the "Time of Jacob's Trouble". "Alas! for that day is great, so that none is like it; it is even the time of Jacob's trouble, but he shall be saved out of it." (Jeremiah 30:7 KJV)

These will truly be "Terrible Days" for the Jewish people. They will be terrible days for all. "The great day of the Lord is near, near and hastening fast; the sound of the day of the Lord is bitter, the mighty man cries aloud there. A day of wrath is that day, a day of distress and anguish, a day of ruin and devastation, a day of darkness and gloom, a day of clouds and thick darkness, a day of trumpet blast and battle cry against fortified cities and against the lofty battlements. . . I will bring distress on men. . . because they have sinned against the Lord, their blood shall be poured out like dust, and their flesh like dung." (Zephaniah 1:14-17 RSV)

Leviticus 23:24 speaks of a blasting of trumpets (plural). That is because there will be two trumpets sounded. One trumpet will be a signal to those of us who love the Lord Jesus that it is time to gather together and be with Him. The other trumpet signals a sound of alarm to the world and particularly to the unbelieving Jewish people who refused their Messiah.

I believe that the Bible teaches there will be seven years of Tribulation for the world. I believe this based on a prophecy in the book of Daniel chapter 9 verses 24 through 27. Daniel and the Jewish people had been taken captive to Babylonia about 600 B.C. Jerusalem had been destroyed. It was while in Babylon that Daniel was given this prophecy. The prophecy states specifically how many years God had decreed upon the Jewish people before He would establish His kingdom on earth and bring about righteousness. That number of years started counting down "from the going forth of the word to restore and build Jerusalem. . ." The decree to rebuild Jerusalem came "in the month of Nisan, in the twentieth year of Artaxerxes the King". (Nehemiah 2:1 Scof.)

This prophecy in Daniel also tells exactly how many years there would be from the proclamation to rebuild Jerusalem to the first coming of Messiah. Bible scholars who have figured these things out tell us it is exactly as the prophet Daniel said—down to the very day that Jesus came the first time. But there are seven years left of this prophecy to be fulfilled. Jesus' first coming was seven years prior to the end of the decreed Jewish age. There are still seven years remaining of the Jewish age and then God will establish His kingdom. There has been an interval of nearly 2000 years—the Church Age. When the Church is removed from the earth, God's time clock with regard to the Jewish age will start ticking again.

There are, as I said, ten days between Rosh Hashana and Yom Kippur and not seven. I wondered about this for several years. Why "Ten Terrible Days"? Why not "Seven Terrible Days" since there are seven years of Tribulation? I believe God has a reason for everything He does. Putting ten days between the Feast of Trumpets and Yom Kippur was no accident. But why?

I finally got down to business with the Lord about this question when I got down to this chapter. I wanted an answer. When we're determined and really seek the Lord for something, He always comes through and He did this time too.

God is showing us something in the symbolism of these ten days. He is not interested in pinpointing the exact number of years involved in the Tribulation in this particular portion of Scripture in Leviticus 23. Rather, the Lord is giving us a picture of what is ultimately happening here on earth while Christians are with the Lord in Heaven. The number "10" in Bible numerology is the number for world activity; it is the number for political consummation and responsibility. In other words, there will be a concentration of world activity during this time. There will be all kinds of activity on the earth. Wars will take place; man's inhumanity and hatred for his fellow man will abound; governments will come to an end. Politics as we know it today will be no more at the end of the Tribulation. God will have allowed man to promote his own program without restraint. In so doing, men will fail miserably. The complete depravity of man will come to the surface.

There will be a world dictator who is motivated by Satan. He will rise to power after God has removed His people (the Church) from the earth. This dictator will thumb his nose at

God and say "I am god". People will follow him and they will bow to his dictates. They will have to follow him in order to get food and jobs. They will be deceived by this dictator. People will even worship him as god. During the seven years of the Tribulation when this dictator (or anti-Christ) will reign, there will be wars and sickness, bloodshed and death, famine and pestilence. There will be so much suffering.

In the end, this dictator will bring his armies against Jerusalem and the Jewish people. He will be defeated by Jesus in the greatest battle ever fought in the valley of Megiddo. This is the Battle of Armageddon. The anti-Christ will then be thrown into the Lake of Fire. The world governments of man will be no more.

This, in brief, is what will be taking place on earth during the Tribulation of which the "Ten Terrible Days" of the Jewish people speak. It is a bleak story, and it is true. But, praise God, there is hope!

If anything has been written here which frightens you, perhaps you don't have the assurance that when the trumpet sounds, you will be among those who will be gathered to meet the Lord. The trumpet of the Feast of Trumpets need not be a sound of alarm to you. It's not too late. You can bow your head right now and ask Jesus to save you from your sins, to become Lord of your life and to keep you from the wrath to come.

God is love. He loves you and wants you to be with Him in Paradise when He sounds the trump of the Feast of Trumpets.

THE DAY OF ATONEMENT

"And the Lord said to Moses, 'On the tenth day of this seventh month is the day of atonement; it shall be for you a time of holy convocation, and you shall afflict yourselves and present an offering by fire to the Lord. And you shall do no work on this same day; for it is a day of atonement, to make atonement for you before the Lord your God. For whoever is not afflicted on this same day shall be cut off from his people. And whoever does any work on this same day, that person I will destroy from among his people. You shall do no work: It is a statute for ever throughout your generations in all your dwellings. It shall be to you a sabbath of solemn rest, and you shall afflict yourselves; on the ninth day of the month beginning at evening, from evening to evening shall you keep your sabbath.'"

Leviticus 23:26-32 RSV

"On the tenth day of this seventh month is the day of atonement". The Feast of Trumpets is on the first day of the seventh month (the month of Tishri). Then comes the "Ten Terrible Days". After those ten days comes Yom Kippur, the Day of Atonement, a very solemn day for the Jewish people. This is actually not a feast day, but a fast day. The Jewish people afflict their bodies on Yom Kippur by fasting the entire day, from sun down to sun down.

79

In the town in which we live, the Jewish people as a whole are not very religious. Many do not go to temple except on special occasions. But even here in New City, on Yom Kippur, you can feel the solemnity that grips the Jewish people. They do not eat. They do not work. They will go to temple for services on this day. The Jewish people have a great wit, but on this day every year, that wit is not displayed. It is a very solemn day.

I have quoted the Scripture from Leviticus 23 which describes Yom Kipper. But there is a much more detailed description of the Day of Atonement found in Leviticus 16. On this day of the year, the high priest had to first sacrifice a bull for his own sins (Leviticus 16:6) and then go into the Holy of Holies with the blood of the bull and a censer of incense. There, in the Holy of Holies, he sprinkled the blood of the bull on the mercy seat for his sins and those of his household.

When the high priest came back out to the people, he would kill one of two goats. The blood of that goat would be taken into the Holy of Holies and sprinkled on the mercy seat for the sins of the people. After sprinkling the blood of the bull and goat as elaborated on in Leviticus 16, the high priest would come out again to the people and lay his hands on the remaining living goat and confess the sins of the people over this goat. Then the goat would be turned out into the wilderness carrying the sins of the people on his head.

Again, because the Temple in Jerusalem was destroyed in 70 A.D., these sacrifices are no longer possible. Therefore, the Jewish people commemorate Yom Kippur by prayer and fasting. They believe the fast puts them in an attitude of humility and repentence. They also believe that by fasting they are sacrificing of themselves by the fat they lose. Since they pray and fast, and since many have done good deeds during the previous ten days, they hope their sins have been forgiven.

The Day of Atonement prophetically points forward to the national Day of Atonement when "all Israel will be saved; as it is written, 'the Deliverer will come from Zion, he will banish ungodliness from Jacob;' 'and this will by my covenant with them when I take away their sins'." (Romans 11:26, 27 RSV)

In the last chapter on the Feast of Trumpets, I explained briefly some of the horrors of the Tribulation. God will pour out His wrath on this sinful world which has refused to accept His way to forgiveness of sins through the blood of Jesus. The world will have gotten progressively more evil and vile in its human nature. God's wrath will be in the form of famine, pestilence, sickness and other "natural" and "supernatural" phenomena. There indeed will be much suffering. Anti-Christ, the Dictator, will bring great persecution upon the Jewish people and also upon the Christians (those who accept Jesus during the Tribulation period). It will be a terrible time to be alive.

But there will be some good also. The Church of Jesus, the Messiah, will be taken out of the earth at the time of the Rapture. At that time God will reveal Himself and His Son to 144,000 Jewish people, 12,000 from each of the twelve tribes of Israel. (Revelation 7:1-8). These Jewish people will realize for the first time Who Jesus is. The Bible tells us that these 144,000 Jews will be appointed as missionaries of God to the lost and dying world in which they live. They will be like 144,000 Apostle Pauls, zealously carrying out their mission for their Lord.

Many people, both Jew and Gentile, will hear the Good News of Jesus' love from these Jewish missionaries and some will believe. These new Christians (Jews and Gentiles) will undergo great persecution during this time of the Tribulation from Anti-Christ. Because of their new faith in Jesus, they will refuse to accept Anti-Christ's mark on their hand or forehead. This mark will be required of all of Anti-Christ's followers. Without it people will not be able to get jobs or buy food. Those without the mark will be outcasts.

The unbelieving Jewish people will also be persecuted by Anti-Christ, who will be possessed by Satan. Satan has tried to destroy God's Ancient People for thousands of years. Haman tried to get rid of the Jewish people in Persia at the time of Queen Esther. Hitler tried it in Europe during World War II. Many others in history have attempted to destroy the Jews, but God has always preserved His people because His redemptive plan for mankind revolves around them and because He still loves them. The Bible tells us that the Jewish people are beloved of God "for the sake of their forefathers". (Romans 11:28)

Jewish people at the time of the Tribulation will be forced back to the land of Israel because of the persecution they will be suffering in every land in which they live. Anti-Christ, that greatest of all dictators, will organize all the armies of the world to descend on Israel. Their commission will be to totally destroy the Jewish nation for once and for all. All the armies of the world will gather to do battle against Jerusalem. And when the Jewish people reach their darkest hour in history, Jesus, their Messiah, will come to them and save them from certain death and destruction by Satan.

The Bible tells us that Jesus will return to the Mount of Olives at the end of the Great Tribulation "and I will pour upon the house of David, and upon the inhabitants of Jerusalem, the Spirit of grace and of supplications; and they shall look upon me whom they have pierced, and they shall mourn for him, as one mourneth for his only son, and shall be in bitterness for him, as one that is in bitterness for his firstborn. In that day shall there be a great mourning in Jerusalem...". (Zechariah 12:10-11 KJV)

"Behold, he (Jesus) is coming with the clouds, and every eye will see him, every one who pierced him; and all tribes of the earth will wail on account of him. Even so, Amen." (Revelation 1:7 RSV)

The Bible tells us in no uncertain terms that the Jewish people who are remaining on earth at the end of the Tribulation will look upon Jesus as He returns to earth to set up His millenial kingdom. They will repent of their sins. They will mourn for Jesus "as one mourneth for his only son" because they have vehemently rejected Him for so long—He Who died for them.

It has been a long time since the Jewish people have really been at one with their God. Jesus came as their eternal atonement by His sacrifice on the cross. But the Jewish people as a nation rejected Him. Then in 70 A.D. the Temple in Jerusalem was totally destroyed. God allowed this because it was no longer necessary for sacrifices to be made in the Temple. The Sacrifice of all ages had been made about 40 years earlier on Calvary. Any other sacrifices were needless and empty. But for those Jewish people who did not accept Jesus' sacrifice, the destruction of the Temple by the Romans left them without even hope of reaching God.

Now at the end of time, as Jerusalem is about to be destroyed and all Israel with her, God will send their Messiah again, to the Mount of Olives. This time God will open their eyes and their hearts to Him Whom they pierced and they will weep. They will repent and believe and they will be saved.

Many Jewish people are already back in the land of their Fathers. They are going back to Israel at this time for many reasons — their reasons. Some are patriotic and want a Jewish homeland. Others are going back to Israel because they have no place else to go. But God has purposed that the Jewish people should return to Israel for a rendezvous with their Messiah. This rendezvous will culminate years of wandering and suffering for Israel. This rendezvous will become their Day of Atonement.

The meaning of the word "atonement" can be broken down in the word itself. "At one ment". Israel for the first time in thousands of years will be "at one" with their God when Jesus reveals Himself to them. The Jewish nation will have found their Messiah at long last. Then they will bow down before Him and worship Him. On that day the sins of the nation will be taken away to the wilderness forever. The "Day of Atonement" will have found its prophetic fulfillment!

THE FEAST OF SUCCOTH

"And the Lord said to Moses, 'Say to the people of Israel, On the fifteenth day of this seventh month and for seven days is the feast of booths to the Lord. On the first day shall be a holy convocation; you shall do no laborious work. Seven days you shall present offerings by fire to the Lord; on the eighth day you shall hold a holy convocation and present an offering by fire to the Lord; it is a solemn assembly; you shall do no laborious work.'"

Leviticus 23:33-36 RSV

Succoth is the Feast of Tabernacles or Booths. It is a beautiful feast; it is a very happy and joyous time. It is said to be the celebration of the end of the harvest season.

Booths or little rooms are built in back of the homes of the religious Jewish people for this occasion. Hung from the ceiling and walls of these rooms are fruits and fresh produce, and leafy boughs of trees. This makes the booth a very colorful, pleasant smelling room.

During the Feast of Tabernacles, as we drive through the Orthodox area of the county in which we live, we can see these booths behind the homes. If the family has a deck off the back of the house, they will put their booth up there. During these eight feast days all of the meals are eaten in the booths (succoth). Each booth has a slatted roof so that the sky can be seen by day and the stars at night. This is a glorious time for the

Jewish families as they spend many hours together in these beautiful cozy rooms. There is a noticeable difference between the solemnity of the previous two feasts and the gaiety and joy of the Feast of Succoth.

The Feast of Booths of the Future

After Jesus physically returns to earth at the end of the Tribulation period, He will set up His millenial kingdom right here on earth. It is from Jerusalem that Jesus will reign.

"It shall come to pass in the latter days that the mountain of the house of the Lord shall be established as the highest of the mountains, and shall be raised up above the hills; the peoples shall flow to it, and many nations shall come, and say: 'Come, let us go up to the mountain of the Lord, to the house of the God of Jacob; that he may teach us his ways and we may walk in his paths.' For out of Zion shall go forth the law, and the word of the Lord from Jerusalem. He shall judge between many peoples, and shall decide for strong nations afar off; and they shall beat their swords into plowshares, and their spears into pruning hooks; nation shall not lift up sword against nation, neither shall they learn war any more; but they shall sit every man under his vine and under his fig tree, and none shall make them afraid; for the mouth of the Lord of hosts has spoken." (Micah 4:1-4 RSV)

You can see from this Scripture in Micah that Jesus will rule and reign from Jerusalem in the "latter days". From there the Word of the Lord will go forth. People from all over will go to Jerusalem to be taught of the Lord. Peace will be upon the world, because the Prince of Peace reigns and Satan is bound.

It is interesting to note that the Feast of Tabernacles is one of the three feasts which required all Jewish males to go up to Jerusalem to sacrifice in the Temple. The prophet Micah speaks of the people flowing up to Jerusalem during the millenial kingdom to be with Jesus.

You can also see in this Scripture a picture of the Feast of Tabernacles as it is celebrated today. The prophet Micah said, "they shall sit every man under his vine and under his fig tree".

The Bible itself tells us that the Feast of Booths speaks of the millenium. "Then every one that survives of all the nations that have come against Jerusalem shall go up year after year to worship the King, the Lord of hosts, and to keep the feast of booths. And if any of the families of the earth do not go up to Jerusalem to worship the King, the Lord of hosts, there will be no rain upon them. And if the family of Egypt do not go up and present themselves, then upon them shall come the plague with which the Lord afflicts the nations that do not go up to keep the feast of booths. This shall be the punishment to Egypt and the punishment to all the nations that do not go up to keep the feast of booths." (Zechariah 14:16-19 RSV)

This will be a joyous time of peace on earth when Jesus, the King of Kings and Lord of Lords, will be physically on earth once more tabernacling with His people in Jerusalem. There will be no sickness, no wars, no anger, no famines, no muggings. The earth will have been brought back full cycle to the state in which it was always meant to be before man fell into sin.

The Numbers Game

My husband was reading through some of the rough drafts I'd made for "God's Blueprint for Mankind". In the Feast of Rosh Hashana, Emil saw my comments regarding the ten days between Rosh Hashana and the Day of Atonement. We hadn't discussed why there were ten days between these two feasts nor had I mentioned to him how the Lord showed me this speaks of world activities. I believe Emil was pleasantly surprised when he read it. But then he challenged, "Well, if that's true, why are there five days between the Day of Atonement and the Feast of Tabernacles?" I was afraid he'd ask me that!

I began to pray and look for books on Bible numerology. I finally obtained a book from a local pastor which had a short chapter on numerology. But the book didn't help. The author was so abstract on his explanation of the number "5" that I didn't understand what he said.

Then one day a Hebrew-Christian friend of ours, Jay Stern, came for dinner. In the course of conversation I made a quip to Emil about his five sermons. (Poor Emil. He's had to put up with a lot from me.) Jay said, "Oh that's alright. That's the number for grace." I'd forgotten Jay had had some Bible school!

As our discussion rolled around to Bible numerology, Jay said he didn't like to get too involved in numerology. "After all, sometimes we have to use numbers just to count."

Well, I don't want to get too hung up on numbers and symbolisms either, but there are times when they definitely have meaning and add to our understanding.

The Day of Atonement will bring the Jewish nation back to a right relationship with their God. Then God will bring His grace upon the whole creation. The lion will lie down with the lamb and there will be harmony in the world at long last. It will be a time when God's grace and mercy will abound for all mankind.

There is significance to the eight day holiday of Tabernacles too. The number "8" speaks of "New Beginnings". Certainly we can see in the millenial age a time of new beginnings for God's creation. The world has been in a state of turmoil and decay since man turned his back on God and Adam decided to do his own thing. "For the creation waits with eager longing for the revealing of the sons of God; for the creation was subjected to futility, not of its own will but by the will of him who subjected it in hope; because the creation itself will be set free from its bondage to decay and obtain the glorious liberty of the children of God." (Romans 8:19-21 RSV)

The Jewish People and The Millenium

As was mentioned before, all of the Feasts of the Lord deal primarily with the Jewish people and this one is no exception. When Jesus returns to earth after the Tribulation, He will return with His saints. "Saint" sounds like a pretty pious word, but it is a Bible term which means anyone who has a personal relationship with Jesus. That means I am a saint! And you are also, if you know the Lord. So when Jesus returns with His saints, that will mean everyone who had been previously raptured. Those saints who died during the Tribulation will be resurrected to life (Revelation 20:4). Then all of the saints together will rule with Jesus from Jerusalem.

But what about the Jewish people? Those who survived the Tribulation will be saved at once when they look upon Him whom they pierced, (Zechariah 12:10) "And so all Israel will be saved" (Romans 11:26).

So the new Jewish saints along with the Jewish saints who died during the Tribulation and those who had been raptured before the Tribulation shall rule with their Messiah along with the Gentile saints.

Why did I say that the Feast of Tabernacles deals primarily with the Jewish people? Because the Bible teaches us that there is a special place or position that the Jewish people will have during the millenial period. "Thus says the Lord of hosts: People shall yet come, even the inhabitants of many cities; the inhabitants of one city shall go to another, saying, 'Let us go at once to entreat the favor of the Lord, and to seek the Lord of hosts; I am going.' Many peoples and strong nations shall come to seek the Lord of hosts in Jerusalem, and to entreat the favor of the Lord. Thus says the Lord of hosts: In those days ten men from the nations of every tongue shall take hold of the robe of a Jew, saying, 'Let us go with you, for we have heard that God is with you'." (Zechariah 8:20-23 RSV)

Joseph and the Sons of Israel

Earlier in "God's Blueprint for Mankind" I mentioned that God gives us types which give us pictures of His plan of salvation. Most of these types speak of Jesus. But others speak of events and, of course, the Feasts of the Lord speak of God's over all plan to redeem the world.

Joseph is an excellent type of Jesus. Joseph was one of the twelve sons of Jacob, whose name is also Israel. Joseph was sold into Egypt as a slave by his brothers. He became the slave of Potiphar and as a servant, he was honest and a blessing to his master. Yet, because he was obedient to God and refused to compromise his beliefs, he wound up in prison.

Finally, Joseph's ability to interpret dreams was made known to Pharaoh. Joseph was given the opportunity to explain the meaning of Pharaoh's dreams. In so doing he became ruler in the land of Egypt. Joseph shows us Jesus as the suffering servant who became the reigning King.

But the story of Joseph shows us something of the Jewish people also. Joseph's brothers as a group, did not love him. The Jewish people (the sons of Israel) as a nation failed to recognize their Messiah and did not give Him their love.

The brothers of Joseph gave him over to the Gentiles to rid themselves of him. The Jewish people turned Jesus over to the Gentiles to rid themselves of their annoyance also.

Joseph suffered at the hands of his brethren and at the hands of the Gentiles of Egypt. Jesus also suffered at the hands of his Jewish brethren and of the Roman Gentiles.

But Joseph became lord and king over a people who were not his own. He became the ruler of the Egyptians. And Jesus, too, became the Lord and King over a people who were not his own according to the flesh. Jesus rules in the hearts of a new entity—the Church—made up of Gentiles as well as Jews.

Then after a period of famine and depression and dearth over the land, the Sons of Jacob, Joseph's brothers, began seeking for answers to their needs. In their search they went to Egypt. They saw Joseph, but did not recognize him immediately. Finally, after time elapsed and some soul searching was done by his brothers, Joseph revealed himself to them and proved to his brothers his forgiveness of them. Joseph said to his brothers, "As for you, you meant evil against me; but God meant it for good, to bring it about that many people should be kept alive, as they are today." (Genesis 50:20 RSV)

Jesus, as I pointed out, will reveal Himself to His brethren at the end of their terrible time of Tribulation and in their deep need. The Jewish people will fall on their knees before Him just as Joseph's brothers fell down before him. Jesus will speak words of comfort to his brethren according to the flesh as He shows them His love and compassion and forgiveness.

Jesus, too, could say to the Jewish people at that time, "you meant evil against me, but God meant it for good to bring it about that many people should be kept alive, as they are today". It was because of Jesus' atoning death and subsequent resurrection that we who believe are kept alive eternally. The book of Romans says, "As regards the Gospel they (the Jewish people) are enemies of God, for your sake". (Romans 11:28 RSV) It is because of their rejection of Messiah that the door of salvation swung open to the Gentiles. God allowed the Jewish people as a nation to become His enemies for our sake.

After Joseph's brothers were restored to him, they were given a special place in Pharaoh's kingdom, "and take your father and your households, and come to me, and I will give you the best of the land of Egypt, and you shall eat the fat of the land'' (Genesis 45:18); ''settle your father and your brothers in the best of the land:''. (Genesis 47:6 RSV)

Just as Pharoah gave Joseph's brothers the best of the land, so will the Jewish people, the Sons of Israel (or Jacob) come into the special place of favor during the Millenium because they were and are and will continue to be ''beloved for the father's sake''. (Romans 11:28 KJV)

Why should the Jewish people receive a place of prominence and favor with God during the Millenium when the Bible tells us ''For God shows no partiality''? (Romans 2:11) When the Scriptures which say ''God is no respector of persons'' and ''God shows no partiality'' are taken in context we see that it refers to obtaining salvation. There is only one way to God and that is through Jesus. Jewish people who do not accept Jesus will have eternal damnation just like a Gentile who refuses Jesus.

By the same token, those who make Jesus Lord, whether Jew or Gentile, will be saved. God shows no partiality. But God does have an order. God ordered the universe and He ordered nature. I've watched four children grow up right in front of me. I marvel every time at the order and precision of their development. Books have been written on child development. In a normal child that development can be predicted with great accuracy. That's the way God made it.

And God made an order in dealing out punishment and rewards. ''There will be tribulation and distress for every human being who does evil, the Jew first and also the Greek''. (Romans 2:9 RSV) In the chapter on the Feast of Rosh Hashana, I mentioned that the Jewish people will have the worst persecution of the Tribulation. ''But glory and honor and peace for every one who does good, the Jew first and also the Greek''. (Romans 2:10 RSV) God gives glory and honor to the Jew first and also to the Gentile. The Jewish people will have a place of favor during the Millenium and also the Gentile followers of Jesus.

So it is that the Feast of Tabernacles speaks of the millenial kingdom in which peace will be restored to the earth and the

King of Kings will reign from Jerusalem with the saints of God. It will be a time of plenty and joy. It will be a glorious, beautiful time for all and the Jewish people will again be the head as God meant them to be.

In speaking of the Jewish people, the Holy Spirit through Paul says, "So I ask, have they stumbled (regarding the Gospel) so as to fall? By no means! But through their trespass salvation has come to the Gentiles, so as to make Israel jealous. Now if their trespass means riches for the world, and if their failure means riches for the Gentiles, how much more will their full inclusion mean!" (Romans 11:11,12 RSV)

Praise the Lord! Their inclusion will mean great glory for us all. Even so, Lord Jesus, come quickly! Maranatha!

THE QUESTION

For you who do not know Jesus as Lord and Saviour, the culmination of God's redemptive plan is not a happy occasion. The Feast of Tabernacles is enjoyed only by those who are invited, those who are members of God's eternal family.

People who are not in the family of God are destined to eternal judgment. "But as for the cowardly, the faithless, the polluted, as for murderers, fornicators, sorcerers, idolaters, and all liars, their lot shall be in the lake that burns with fire and brimstone, which is the second death." (Revelation 21:8 RSV)

If you have read this book and have not asked Jesus into your life and trusted in His atonement on the cross for your sins, you are now without excuse. You have heard the Word of God. You've been given a free will. No one can force you to do anything. But there is a question before you now. Your answer has eternal consequences. WHAT WILL YOU DO WITH JESUS?

For further information or literature write:

BLESS ISRAEL TODAY®

P.O. Box 39

New City, N.Y. 10956